Franc Bangs Wilkie

Sketches and Notices of the Chicago Bar

Including the More Prominent Lawyers and Judges of the City. Fourth Edition

Franc Bangs Wilkie

Sketches and Notices of the Chicago Bar
Including the More Prominent Lawyers and Judges of the City. Fourth Edition

ISBN/EAN: 9783337018917

Printed in Europe, USA, Canada, Australia, Japan

Cover: Foto ©ninafisch / pixelio.de

More available books at **www.hansebooks.com**

SKETCHES AND NOTICES

OF

THE CHICAGO BAR;

INCLUDING THE MORE PROMINENT

LAWYERS AND JUDGES

OF THE CITY AND SUBURBAN TOWNS.

BY F. B. WILKIE, (POLIUTO.)

FOURTH (REVISED) EDITION.

CHICAGO:
THE WESTERN NEWS COMPANY
1872.

Entered according to Act of Congress, in the year 1871,

BY F. B. WILKIE,

in the office of the Librarian of Congress, at Washington.

PREFACE TO FIRST EDITION.

The subject-matter herewith given, was written for, and published in, THE SUNDAY TIMES of this city. The sketches are now presented in book form, after having received important revision, alteration and addition.

CHICAGO, May, 1871.

PREFACE TO SECOND EDITION.

THE present edition has been made up since the Great Fire, and contains many names and includes much matter that were not in the former edition.

CHICAGO, June, 1872. F. B. W.

I.

WILLIAM K. McALLISTER.

ALTHOUGH Judge McAllister has been recently promoted to the bench of the Supreme Court of Illinois, at the present time of writing it is deemed best to notice him as a lawyer. Up to a very recent date, he has been identified with the legal fraternity; and his character as a lawyer is yet too fresh in the minds of all to permit his being passed over as not belonging to this branch of the legal profession.

Judge McAllister is now about fifty-two years of age, and he was born on a farm, in Salem, Washington county, New York. He remained on the farm until he was about eighteen years of age, when he entered college, and was obliged to leave without graduating, owing to ill health. He then devoted some time to hunting and fishing, and a general out-door life, in order to recuperate. At the age of twenty-one he began the study of law in Wayne county, under a lawyer named Henry, finished his studies in Yates county, and then removed to Albion, where he resided some ten years.

While in Albion he steadily followed his profession, and was brought into contact with some of the best legal minds of the State, and thereby secured an experience and a discipline which, to a young lawyer, were invaluable. In 1854 he came to Chicago, and since that period until his promotion to the Supreme bench, he followed his chosen profession. His official life is easily summed up. He ran against Jameson as a candidate for Judge of the Superior Court in 1866, but was unsuccessful. In 1868 he ran for Judge of the Recorder's Court, and was overwhelmingly elected. In 1870 he was elected a Judge of the Supreme Court, which position he now occupies.

In personal appearance Judge McAllister is attractive. He is of medium height, has a well-rounded figure, and a massive forehead, whose character is not detracted from by the intense humaneness of the face and womanly eyes below. His mouth is small and sensitive, his eyes large, lustrous and blue, and his cheeks clean shaven. There is nothing effeminate in the face, yet it is so fine and kindly that it becomes benignant in some of its expressions. This fineness, this sensitiveness, this warm humanity, are major qualities in his make-up, and are potent in their consequences with reference to every act of his private and his professional life.

As may be inferred, these generous elements in his character very largely influence him in the practice of his profession. He is too kindly to be unjust, too humane to be ever found save on the side which he conscientiously believes to be right. A result of this is that he has always gone before a court or a jury with such a profound conviction of the justice of his cause that this fact alone has carried great weight, and has been a prime element in the success which has attended him.

As a lawyer, he possesses great industry, a very comprehensive knowledge of the law, and a logical ability, the general result of which is that he rarely if ever makes any blunders. His decisions, while on the Recorder's bench, when taken to the Supreme Court, with a single exception, came back sustained. He combines in himself the better qualities of an attorney and an advocate. He can prepare his own brief with a perfection that permits of no flaw, and then try it in so masterly a manner that the success of his client has nearly always been assured when he agrees to accept a retainer. Before a jury, he always was effective from the sincerity before spoken of, and which, with his entire truthfulness, his complete avoidance of anything like trickery or buncombe, his clear knowledge of the case, has given him an eloquence whose power was infinitely in excess of that of any professed and pretentious elocutionist.

No lawyer in Chicago stands higher than Judge McAllister. His integrity, humanity and sincerity have become proverbial; and so high is his personal character, that he has escaped even the attacks of political partizanship. In his private life he is no less elevated than in his professional career. He is fond of the society of personal friends; and when he unbends himself from the official strain he has all the elasticity and freshness of boyhood. He rarely goes into general society, but has intense domesticity, and finds no place so attractive as home, with its luxuries, its music, its affections and its beauties. In fine, whether regarded as an official or a private citizen, Judge McAllister is a gentleman whose intellect is superior, and whose life and motives are absolutely above all reproach.

JOSEPH KNOX.

THIS gentleman belongs to the former generation, but he also belongs to the profession both of Chicago and the West, and therein is entitled to a place in the present group of celebrities. He was born in Blanford, Massachusetts, in 1805. He studied law with his brother, General Alanson Knox, in his native town, and was admitted to the bar in 1828. He then removed to Worcester county, in the same State, and commenced the practice of his profession, and while there was thrown into competition with such men as Hon. John Davis, Rejoice Newton, Charles Allen, Ira Barton, Pliny Merrick and Emory Washburne, all of whom are now dead save the last named.

In 1837 he removed West with his family to Stephenson, now Rock Island county, Illinois, where he continued in the practice of law for twenty-three years. During the most of that period he was associated with Hon. John W. Drury, under the name of Knox & Drury, a firm whose name has been heard and made familiar throughout the entire West. During most of the time, the Rock Island circuit embraced some ten adjacent counties, in addition to practicing in all of which, Mr. Knox's professional labors carried him into Peoria and Knox counties, in which he met such men as Judges Purple and Peters, L. B. Knowlton and Julius Manning, who were his associates or competitors in all these districts, and among whom there sprang into existence a deep personal attachment and intimacy, as was also the case at Rock Island with Judge I. O. Wilkinson, now of Chicago, and his partner, Judge Pleasants.

Mr. Knox removed to Chicago in 1860, and soon after was made State's Attorney, a position which he held for four years, until it passed by election to his then partner, the present incumbent, Charles H. Reed. Since that period, Mr. Knox has been in general practice, and now, although sixty-six years of age, he walks daily a distance of four miles to and from his office, and has not seen a day's illness in thirty years. Mr. Knox is a trifle below medium height, is slender, with gray hair and beard, and blue eyes. His head is large, and filled with a brain of enormous power. His great success in his profession is so well known that more than mere allusion to it here would be superfluous. He is an advocate, and it was said of him by Judge McLean : " He is the most powerful jury advocate I ever had before me."

Among the many highly important cases in which he has been engaged, and the trial of which has made his name prominent on the list of leading lawyers in the West, may be mentioned the trial of the murderers of Colonel Davenport, at Rock Island, in 1846 ; the successful defense, at Iowa City, in 1857, of the nine men charged with the murder of Boyd Wilkinson, and which trial lasted an entire month; the successful defense, in the United States Court held in Chicago by Justice McLean, some twelve years ago, in the case of the owners of the steamer Effie Afton against the Rock Island Bridge Company ; the Frink and Walker case ; the Hopps murder trial ; the case against Judge Scates ; and many others of like importance.

THOMAS HOYNE.

Mr. Hoyne is scarcely now in the active practice of the profession of law. He has had a long and active as well as brilliant career in Chicago and the West as a lawyer, a politician, and an official. Just now he is rather reclining upon his honors, and is bringing to the front members of his own family, whom, in the liberal professions, he proposes to make as prominent as he has been, or is himself. Although somewhat withdrawn from the practice of his chosen profession, he has been so long identified with the bar of Chicago, and the political interests of the West, that an omission of his name in an article of the present character would leave it noticeably incomplete. His life is of value as teaching what may be accomplished by industry and a determination to permit no obstacle to interfere with a rapid progress.

Mr. Hoyne was born in New York city in 1817, and he there attended school until 1830. He was then apprenticed to a manufacturer of fancy goods, and remained at the business until 1835. Having, during his apprenticeship, found time to cultivate his intellect, and the acquaintance of some eminent men, he determined to study law. He worked in a wholesale grocery in the day time and studied at night, during a year. He then entered the law office of Hon. John Brinkerhoff, and remained another year. In 1837 he came to Chicago, then in the first year of its existence under a city charter. He obtained employment in the Circuit Clerk's office, studied hard all the while, taught for a time in one of the public schools, took up Latin and French in addition to law, and in 1839 completed his legal studies in the office of Hon. J. Y. Scammon, and was very soon after admitted to the bar.

From that period down to the present time, Mr. Hoyne has been prominently before the people of Chicago. He was elected City Clerk in 1840, to which office he was reëlected the succeeding year. In 1841 he drew up a memorial to Congress praying for the completion of the harbor of this city—an exhaustive and able document. To this was attached a schedule of all the mercantile firms which had been engaged in business up to that time. This was an undertaking requiring indomitable energy and perseverance, there being at that early day neither Custom House or Board of Trade Registry, in consequence of which all information was obtained by personal application to the parties. At this time the population of Illinois was principally Southern in birth and taste, with strong prejudices against New England habits. Notwithstanding, the Common Council decided to get up a local and pocket edition of Thanksgiving in Chicago, and Mr. Hoyne, as City Clerk, drew up the first proclamation ever issued in Illinois.

He removed to Galena for two years and then returned to Chicago, and was elected Probate Judge in 1847; and after the election of Pierce he was made United States District Attorney for the District of Illinois. In 1859 he was made United States Marshal for the Northern District of this State.

In 1851 he was elected President of the Young Men's Association (late Library Association), which had maintained a precarious existence since 1842, drew up a charter, provided for a building, established a lecture course, and delivered before the society a lecture upon "Trial by Jury." He was reëlected in 1852, the only instance, with one exception, where the same person has held the office two consecutive years.

He was the first to make an effort to establish a law school in this part of the country, and procured at great personal expense the first Professor, the present Judge Booth, beside making a contribution of five thousand dollars as an endowment fund to establish in the University of Chicago a chair of constitutional and international law. He has been an officer of the Institution in various capacities from its organization to the present time. The total destruction of the library and records of the Law Institute in the fire of October, 1871, rendered an immense amount of labor necessary to its reëstablishment. Mr. Hoyne was Chairman of the Committee on Correspondence, in which capacity his untiring efforts were successful in procuring large and valuable contributions from the various States to the library of the Institute. In the work of building up the Chicago University he has been an efficient laborer and a munificent patron. He was an active agent in the purchase of the great telescope, the largest refractor on the globe; and has been Secretary of the Astronomical Society since its organization. He was also, at the time of the destruction of its archives and buildings, Vice-President of the

Historical Society. In fine, in all the monuments of law, literature and politics erected in Chicago, there appear material elements, which are the handiwork of the subject of our sketch.

In other respects Mr Hoyne has been very prominent and active. He has given his personal influence in every national canvass which has occurred since his residence in Chicago. He has been a speaker and writer of incessant activity on every question of importance that has come before the public.

During the war he was, with Judges Drummond, John M. Wilson, Arrington and others, a member of the Union Defense Committee; and it was he who wrote the celebrated address that was issued over the signature of John M. Wilson as chairman. Among his later efforts, his oration at Ottawa, Illinois, on the 4th of July, 1871, on the "New Departure," was a production which added greatly to an already brilliant reputation as an orator. In September of the same year, at the Democratic State Convention, as Chairman of the Committee on Resolutions, he drafted the platform which was adopted, and has since become the basis of the Liberal movement.

As a lawyer, he has occupied a position second to but few, which fact, in connection with his vast labors in other directions, proves his great industry and his high ability. Among the notable trials in which he has been engaged, are the celebrated Bush case; and a litigation involving nearly half a million of dollars, which he brought to a successful termination in favor of his client.

In personal appearance Mr. Hoyne is a very marked man. His eyes are black and piercing, his countenance swarthy, his features regular, and his hair jet black and curly. He is erect, rather haughty in his carriage, and resembles more than anything else, an intellectual and aristocratic outgrowth of southern Europe. His appearance is changing, sometimes being sunny and genial, and at other times haughty and *distrait*, with a hint of savagery, as if he were about going on the war-path. He is a man of an irascible disposition, but who, while quick to resent, is equally ready to pardon, or to confess an error when one has been committed. He is eminently chivalrous in all his feelings, and is one of the most thorough and finished gentlemen at the Chicago bar. He is impulsive to a very high degree, and while acting from these motives is always prepared to review his course in his cooler moments, and to pronounce as dispassionately with reference to himself as to another. He is thoroughly respected, not only as a lawyer, but as a citizen. His quick, impetuous nature inclines him to warm attachments; and he is one whose positive views of everybody incline him either to like or dislike everything with which he comes in contact. He is indifferent in his regard to but few people whom he knows, and for this reason he includes everybody among his friends or enemies. That the latter are the few, and the former the many, is proof positive of his geniality and his just discrimination of character. In his life he has furnished a model which every young man of Chicago can study and imitate with profit.

WILLIAM C. GOUDY.

THIS gentleman was born in Indiana in 1824, and eight years afterward removed to Illinois, and has resided here ever since. He graduated at the Illinois College in 1845, and read law at Springfield under Judge S. T. Logan. He began his professional career in 1848 in Fulton county, and remained there until 1860. During this period he practiced in several adjacent counties of the Military Tract, in the Supreme Court, and the United States Court of Springfield. He was a partner of Judge Wead, now of Peoria, until that gentleman was elected Judge in 1853. When he commenced practice he encountered Archibald Williams, O. H. Browning, Julius Manning, Judge Purple, Chief Justice Lawrence, Cyrus Walker, Thomas L. Harris, the late President Lincoln, and other distinguished lawyers of central Illinois, and in that school was compelled to triumph or fail. His progress was rapid, so that he was the acknowledged leader of that portion of the bar when he made this city his home. In 1856 he was sent to the State Senate from the counties of Fulton and McDonough, and he served the State in this legislative capacity for four years. From 1852 to 1855 he was State's Attorney of the Tenth Judicial District, but resigned his office to give his attention more largely to civil practice.

The positions of Senator and State's Attorney are the only official ones Mr. Goudy has ever held, although he has been presented for other offices. He was a candidate for United States Senator in 1863, and the year before was also a candidate for the Constitutional Convention, but was unsuccessful in both cases. At the close of 1859 he removed to Chicago, since which he has resided here, and has practiced his profession in the Federal and State Courts, and also in the Supreme Court at Washington. The reports of the Supreme Court of Illinois show Mr. Goudy to have been an extensive practitioner from 1853 to the present time, and his cases may be found in every volume of the forty volumes since he argued his first case before that tribunal. There is no practitioner in the State who has had a greater number of cases before the Supreme Court than Mr. Goudy, and of these many are of the greatest importance. In closing this outline of his public life, it may be added that Mr. Goudy once took an active personal interest in politics; and while doing so achieved a reputation second to no amateur politician in Illinois. Latterly he has totally abandoned politics, and he now devotes himself exclusively to his profession.

Mr. Goudy is of medium height and build. He has blue or gray eyes and regular features, whose expression when in repose, or in the presence of strangers, would seem to rather repel intimacy. Still, sometimes in conversation, or during the delivery of a speech, the face lights up and glows, and then becomes genial, expressive and inviting.

As a general practitioner and real estate lawyer, Mr. Goudy takes no second position at the Chicago bar. He wastes no words in presenting a case, but goes directly to the point, and holds himself to it until the subject is completely exhausted. Thoroughly posted on authorities, he presents them clearly and in logical order; and thus, while scarcely ever rhetorically brilliant, he is thoroughly effective. His opinions on real estate matters are the result of an extended knowledge of authorities, an intimate acquaintance with the routine and practice involved in such business, and an observation sharpened by long experience. He unravels without seeming difficulty the most intricate questions, and patiently but surely reaches conclusions that are rarely other than sound and complete.

One of his marked qualities is an intense secretiveness. He is reticent, and is always a sort of locomotive enigma. In the preparation of a charter or legislative act, he evinces vast foresight, and in any litigation which may grow from any such charter or acts, he is able, with almost entire certainty, to anticipate the decision of the higher courts. As a counsellor he is a very prudent man, and he will never give a client an opinion that will be likely to involve him in a losing litigation. He prepares a case with the utmost care, tries it closely, discusses legal questions arising with great clearness, is perfectly unmoved during its progress, and accepts defeat or victory with a passionless face and an imperturbability that are adamantine in their character.

In his private life Mr. Goudy is characterized by a large development of domestic qualities of a high order. He has acquired a fortune from the practice of his profession, and possesses a home to whose adornment he gives all the time which can be spared from his office life. He is a competent lawyer, a respected citizen, and a gentleman who fully appreciates and enjoys the comforts of a luxurious home.

CORYDON BECKWITH.

THIS gentleman was born in Vermont in 1823. He was educated in Providence, Rhode Island, and in Brentham, Massachussetts. He studied law in St. Albans, Vermont, and was admitted to the bar of that place in 1844; and two years later he was admitted to the bar of Maryland. He commenced the practice of law in St. Albans in 1847, and remained there until 1853, when he removed to Chicago. Since residing here he served a limited term on the Supreme bench, having been appointed to that position by Governor Yates.

In personal appearance, Judge Beckwith is not what would be considered an Adonis, although his looks indicate intellect and energy. He is of very substantial build, with a large, well-balanced head, prominent and large black eyes, a swarthy complexion, black hair, and a clean-shaved face. His whole appearance suggests strength, resolution and secresy. His face is strong rather than refined; and his mental characteristics seem the reflection of his massive, strong-built physical organization. He is more of the weaver's beam, the pile-driving class of mechanicism than that of a music-box.

In his mental development, Judge Beckwith is a remarkable man. He is universally conceded to be, in many essential particulars, the very strongest lawyer at this bar. As a lawyer, he has very profound learning. He is one who is governed by principles, and not cases. He is a man who always presents what he has to offer to a court and jury in a novel and forcible manner. He is, perhaps, less a mere advocate than some others in the profession; but his chief ability lies in a different and higher direction. It is entirely safe to say of him that, as an opponent, he is the most dangerous lawyer in the West.

Perhaps there is no member of the legal profession in this city whom it is not more easy to accurately describe than Judge Beckwith. He is, above all things, reticent and secretive, and is none the less so than at times, when necessity demands, he seems boyishly frank, and ingenuously communicative. He has the frankness of a Talleyrand, who communicates to one just what he desires to say, and no more. It is for this reason that a faithful description of him is a matter of supreme difficulty. One does not always know him, who apparently is in a position to know him best. These peculiarities are not asserted to be a defect in his composition; they may be, and undoubtedly are, a necessary development of his character as a great manager.

It is as a manager, a director of operations, that he assumes a grand position. He is a man who can originate a line of offense or defense better, probably, than any lawyer in Chicago. He has also the ability to execute; but perhaps this quality in his character does not receive the recognition it deserves, for various reasons. Principally is this the case from the fact that he is oftener called upon to plan than to carry out what he has designed. He is somewhat in the position of a leader of a great army whose *corps d'armee* are operating over an extended country. In such a case, the leader is not called on to execute. He directs movements, and leaves their execution to subordinates. Constantly consulted in cases of all kinds, by all classes, and more especially by lawyers, Judge Beckwith devises operations for them, lays out the plan of carrying them through, and then leaves the minutiæ to their action. From this fact has grown the impression that he can not execute, whereas the truth is that he has demonstrated the exact contrary in many cases, while it is further true that he has not the time to, nor is there a necessity for, his devoting himself to details. It may also be added that he is often the hidden inspiration in many a case in which others appear as the prominent figures, while they are in reality but instruments, moved by wires whose termination and moving power are not seen or suspected by the public.

The inference is unavoidable from this statement, that he acts frequently by indirection. This is true. He seems to often prefer this method of attack and defense. It leaves the real origin of the forces in operation a mystery, and therein baffles those against whom they are directed. From this fact may have grown the impression that he is a lobbyist in politics; but in this respect it is entirely safe to say that he is not a success, whatever may be his aspirations in that direction. He may occasionally be seen about the outer circle of the halls of legislation, but, whatever he may desire there, or whatever may be his success, it is certain that he belongs to judicial rather than legislative departments, and that his true *rôle* is that of the legal manager. In this line of effort he has few rivals and no superior. He is not only a very profound lawyer, but he is a diplomatic lawyer in addition. He adds to his exhaustive knowledge of law, a thorough knowledge of all its mechanism, of human nature — such as may be required to be operated upon in a legal direction — and of all the appliances which must be employed to achieve success.

Present defeat does not baffle, nor does a sudden, unexpected and pressing emergency unnerve or discompose him. He is so fertile in invention, and so experienced in details, that nothing can find him unprepared, or throw him from his balance. He has not only a great legal mind, but he has the mind, the secretiveness, the resolution, the nerve of a diplomat. He can not only operate all the tremendous machinery of law, but he can bring to its aid, in any desired direction, the powerful mechanism of secret influences, remote personal efforts, and a complication of agencies, that are the more potential in that they are invisible, and almost always unsuspected. Men who have him as an opponent, have not merely to combat the lawyer who is familiar with all principles and precedents, and rules of practice, but also a supreme and sagacious management, whose character and power are never known until the moment of their development. There is no more industrious member of the legal profession than Judge Beckwith, and there rarely occurs a case of more than average importance in which he is not retained. He excels in the preparation of condensed, pertinent briefs, and in the handling of cases in which there are no precedents, and in which he originates or discovers the legal principles necessary to their successful disposition. As an originator he is just as remarkable as he is a manager, and in both these respects he probably stands without a rival.

Socially, Judge Beckwith is very agreeable. His knowledge of men is vast, and in this he possesses a never-ending fund of interesting information. He is much liked by those who are intimate with him, and he adds to his personal popularity the renown of being among the very first lawyers, not merely of Chicago, but of the country. ' He is a man of very generous impulses and actions, is large-hearted and large-souled, and his kindness to young lawyers has not only been frequent, but it has been of material value to them, and forms a subject to very many of them of grateful remembrance.

SAMUEL W. FULLER.

THIS lawyer is one of those men who are popularly known as self-made. He has risen to his present position, not by the aid of wealth, or of great natural abilities, but by a perseveringly studious life, and entire dependence upon himself for the means to secure his educational advancement.

He is now about forty-eight years of age, and is a native of Vermont, where he was admitted to the bar and married. He came to this State with only his education and his hands, and supported himself for a while as school-teacher, until he could secure practice as a lawyer. It was while he was thus combining the pedagogue and the lawyer, that he resided in Tazewell county, in this State. He was there admitted to the bar, and from that place he was sent to the Illinois Senate, where his abilities first attracted the notice of J. Y. Scammon, with whom Mr. Fuller is now in partnership. In time, he came where a majority of all the great lawyers of the Northwest come, to Chicago. The distance between the Tazewell county school-teacher and the prominent member of the law firm of Scammon, McCagg & Fuller, is broad, and that it has been traversed in comparatively so short a space of time, is in the highest degree complimentary to the endurance and perseverance of the gentleman whose name heads this article.

In personal appearance Mr. Fuller is a study. He is tall, slender, with sandy whiskers and moustache, light gray eyes, a very broad and prominent forehead, and abundant hair. His countenance is as fine as a proof, and has the delicacy of a close-worked steel engraving. It is a face whose salient indications are refinement, intelligence, and a sort of timid diffidence that is almost girlish. It is a face which, in addition to these indications, shadows forth a singularly legible expression of honesty and candor. Were one to conclude from the study of the face that its owner were a clergyman, or a literary man,—as he probably would,—he would think that it had no failure; but were he told that its possessor were a lawyer, he might be of the opinion that a few coarser lines in it would be of advantage. In brief, it is rather too fine a face for the popular estimate of the character of a lawyer. It would do for some scientist, who requires patient investigation, and not imagination, or for any other class of professional men who do not need any inherent driving power, and whose business is of a character that demands no enthusiasm, only a calm and undeviating appreciation.

The mental processes of Mr Fuller are slow, and remarkably correct and sure. He has a very excellent knowledge of law, but not sufficient to make him devoted to its letter in contra-distinction to its spirit. He has a very thorough comprehension of legal principles, and the knowledge of books requisite to give those principles authoritative force. His *rôle* is not that of an advocate to any considerable extent. His presentation of a case is never fervid, or forcible in a rhetorical sense. Nevertheless, his comprehension of principles and authorities, together with a clear habit of thought, enables him to present a case with great logical force. If he has a failure in his character as an advocate before a jury, it is found in the fact that he seems to over-estimate their intelligence. He addresses them with the terseness that he would employ were he addressing a judge, or men of his own intellectual level. He will present them a point in the fewest possible words, and then leave it. He never *insists* upon their comprehending it. He does not amplify it, and present it to them in different lights, as should be done in the case of a jury of men of ordinary capacity, and of whom no two can, by any possibility, see the same thing from the same point of view. Either Mr. Fuller pays the jury too high a compliment in intentionally confining his statements to mathematical brevity and precision, or else he commits a blunder in not better comprehending the necessities of the situation occupied by a jury lawyer. His addresses have all the nakedness of mathematical propositions. They never glow or melt, but they convince, providing they are given to minds that have the capacity to comprehend his statements, and the honesty to decide according to their convictions. He presents his propositions calmly and modestly, but rather in the style of a clear-headed collegiate professor, enunciating propositions of a high order to men of his own profession. He knows no such thing as engineering or figuring a case. He regards it from a standpoint which includes the legal principle, the evidence, and the interests of his clients. If he wins a case, it is done straight-forwardly, and upon its merits, and if he conducts his case in such a manner that he is defeated, he always retires with the honors of war and the entire respect of his opponents.

Mr. Fuller strengthens himself as a thinker, and adds elements of dignity to his mental character by an indulgence in the better class of literary productions. He is a reader and a thinker outside of his profession. He is not a good manager in the sense of conducting the financial affairs connected with his professional services, and herein he is most admirably complemented by one of his partners, E. B. McCagg, who is himself a lawyer of very great ability, and who is a close business man, and who carefully gathers up the raveled financial threads which are upon the fringe of Mr. Fuller's professional actions. These two men are admirably adapted to each other. Mr. McCagg has a very thorough knowledge of the world, which Mr. Fuller has not; and in this, as in various other ways, he assists in giving the firm a roundness and completeness of great perfection. In many respects he contrasts beneficially with Mr. Fuller. He is, as has been said, practical in directions where the other displays no particular ability; he is a close business man, a good collector, and withal, just enough cynical to relieve the unvarying quietness and unruffled affability of the other.

Mr. McCagg is also a noted man in other respects. He is possessed of great wealth, and he lives in a style whose luxuriance has few or no equals in Chicago. He has a large amount of public spirit, has a great number of very excellent qualities whose possession secures him a universal and very thorough respect. Mentally he is in no respect the inferior of Mr. Fuller, and were he obliged to resort to the more public practice of his profession he would be a successful advocate as well as what he now is, a sound and careful lawyer. The two, however, pull well together, and while both have an abundance of positive qualities in a high order of excellence, each supplies a certain class of equally desirable qualities which the other lacks; or presents such a combination of characteristics that each modifies, brings out, or otherwise improves those of the other. The Hon. J. Y. Scammon is still the senior member of the firm, and while now giving no attention to the law, he has a high reputation as a lawyer which remains to him as a consequence of a highly successful career. Mr. Scammon's entire time is occupied with the care of private interests which are enormous; but his reputation as a superior lawyer, and his wealth, social consequence, and extended commercial relations, are well reflected in the firm of which himself and McCagg and Fuller are members.

ROBERT HERVEY.

MR. HERVEY was born in Glasgow, Scotland, in 1820, and was educated at the grammer school and university of the same city. He graduated in 1837, and studied law in Toronto with Hon. Henry Sherwood, formerly Attorney-General of Canada, and was admitted to the Canadian bar in 1842. He practiced in Ottawa, Canada, for ten years, and in 1852 removed to Chicago, and was the partner of Judge Morris until 1856.

In personal appearance Mr. Hervey is rather *distingué*. His form is medium height, very erect and well proportioned. His complexion is fresh, his whiskers are gray and worn in the English fashion, his hair is silvery, his head well-shaped, his eyes gray and keen, and the *tout ensemble* that of a very pronounced Scotchman. In his demeanor he is very affable and courteous, and before a jury, and in the examination of a witness, as well as in his treatment of opposing counsel, he is always gentlemanly and considerate. He is regarded as well-posted on authorities, and a very competent man, whether in the office or before a jury. He is industrious, careful of the interests of his clients, and conservative in his mental processes.

In his oratory he is dignified, and after warming up he becomes forcible, but never robustious. He rises to a certain moderate height, both of thought and declamation, but his average level is a trifle lower. When under full pressure as a speaker, he has a certain mannerism, which is probably the result of habit, and is not the outgrowth or the inspiration of his thoughts. He then buttons his coat across his well-shaped chest, closes his eyes as if in a rhapsody, thrusts one hand into his bosom, and gracefully emphasizes with the other. His jury efforts are of a good average quality. They are clear, logical, and always given with effective *empressement*.

Socially, Mr. Hervey is quite popular. He is somewhat Chesterfieldian in his manners; and, on the streets is what, in a younger man, might be termed nobby. He is a standing model of a polite, courteous gentleman, and as such he is very generally liked by the members of his profession, by the community at large, and the more especially among his Scotch fellow-citizens, by whom he is regarded as a leading orator and a representative man.

JAMES M. WALKER.

IN many respects Mr. Walker stands at the very head of the legal profession in the West. This refers more especially to the magnitude of the interests which he has been intrusted with, and which include some of the largest corporations in the country. His reputation may not be a popular one, like that of Charles O'Conor, or James Brady; but among great moneyed corporations, and in directions where acquaintance is fame, and esteem a fortune, Mr. Walker is both known and esteemed.

He was born in Claremont, N. H., and is now about fifty years of age. He studied law at Ann Arbor, in Michigan, and began the practice of law at that point. He afterward removed to another portion of Washtenaw county, in the same State, where he speedily secured a very large practice, and filled the office of prosecuting attorney. He removed to Chicago in 1854, at which time he was the attorney of the Michigan Central railway. He first occupied an office with James M. Joy, and later formed a legal connection with Mr. Sedgwick, and subsequently he entered into partnership with Wirt Dexter; and soon after took the position of attorney for the Chicago, Burlington and Quincy railway, which important position he still holds, and it may be added that he is to the Burlington and Quincy railway company what Joy is to the Michigan Central — a very king.

In personal appearance he is slender, of medium height, with a small, active brain, gray eyes, and gray hair and goatee. His countenance bears the evidence of a laborious life. He evidently has more soul than body, and all his life has overdriven the latter in order to execute the demands of the former. In manner he is rather abstracted and reticent, and goes about wrapped in a species of semi-isolation. This is not so much the result of coldness as of the preoccupation of thought.

As a lawyer he occupies a very conspicuous position. His forte lies in the mastering of the great problems connected with corporations; and in this direction he has been eminently successful. Before a jury or a court he does not occupy so elevated a grade, for several reasons, among which is prominent the fact that a man who devotes his entire energies to the mastery of great problems has not the leisure to cultivate the graces and blandishments of oratory. Another reason is possibly found in the additional fact that, as is not uncommon with hard students like himself, he is very pertinacious when he has once formed a conclusion, and is very apt to insist that juries and others shall see the matter at issue in the same light. This trait is conviction and something more. It is rather a positive belief that admits of no contradiction, and is not disposed to accept a difference of opinion. He devotes so much time and strength to the examination of a question that he believes his conclusions are not simple convictions, but they are absolute axioms which must not and cannot be disputed.

Among other of his traits his industry is not the least remarkable. When he once takes hold of a question of importance, it becomes an absorbing one, and to its solution he gives every energy. Nature, time, labor, pain are nothing. He hesitates at no sacrifice, and pushes his investigations till he either reaches their solution or his health gives way under the exertion. Two or three times in his life has he thus driven himself to the verge of the grave by his persistence in labor long after labor had ceased to be a duty or a virtue. Apart from his professional duties he is gentlemanly and considerate. His reading is extensive. He has a very exquisite taste in fine art; his benevolence is very great; and his general information of an extended character. What he lacks is more regard for himself, and a more leisurely performance of the duties of his profession. Were this defect remedied, he would be no less successful than he is and has been, while he would enjoy that physical energy and elasticity without which any existence is incomplete and unsatisfactory.

LEONARD SWETT.

Mr. SWETT was born in Oxford, Maine, in 1825. He graduated at Waterville, and read law at Portland, after which he entered the army and served as a private during the Mexican war. He removed to Bloomington, in this State, in 1849, and was admitted to the bar the same year. At one time he was a member of the legislature, and has been prominently before the public in other capacities. He removed to Chicago in 1865, and has since resided in this city.

In personal appearance Mr. Swett very much resembles the late Abraham Lincoln. He is tall, angular, dark, with prominent features, and in fact he so generally resembles the late Mr. Lincoln that any detailed description of him would be useless. This coincidence with respect to physical similitude extends in a considerable degree to the mental characteristics of the two men. Mr. Swett is more polished than was his antetype; he is more finished, but this makes the difference between them one of degree rather than of kind. He possesses the same class of humor peculiar to the late President, and often employs the same quaint, epigramatic method of expression which was peculiar to Mr. Lincoln, and so familiar to the man. Of course, these resemblances are mere happenings. Neither Mr. Lincoln nor Mr. Swett made a study of each other with a view to imitation. Nor is their anything strange in the coincidence. When one considers how many men there are born every year, the wonder is, not that two men are found who closely resemble each other, but that there are so many varieties in the workmanship.

As a lawyer Mr. Swett takes a very high rank, both in Chicago and the State. In his professional character he possesses a fair allowance of versatility, but his special excellencies lie in the direction of the trial of cases, and, possibly, in the handling of criminal business. He has a very clear, analytical mind, and a very comprehensive view of a subject, and is, therefore, in this respect well fitted for office business. But his tendencies seem to be in the direction of the trial of cases, for the reason, perhaps, that office business brings into activity few or none of the emotional qualities of the soul. Mr. Swett has imagination, humor, pathos, and an abundance of similar qualities whose exercise is as essential to his enjoyment as the use of his muscles is to a strong, vigorous man. It requires a mind from which the warmer qualities have been eliminated, and a mechanism which has been reduced to a mathematical variety of construction, to produce a lawyer who will prefer the investigation of dry authorities to the warmth, the poetry, the excitement, the elasticity, the cunning of a trial. Mr. Swett is an orator; and in this fact is found the explanation of his preference.

As a speaker he has few or no superiors at the bar. He requires scarcely any preparation to make a speech on any subject. He sees a case clearly, and he has the faculty of presenting it with equal clearness. He presents it forcibly because he feels intensely. He has that tendency toward amplification found in all true orators, and by whose aid he presents a single point in so many salient aspects that it becomes as apparent as sunlight to his auditory. This ability to not only clearly present a point, but to restate it and reiterate it under a slightly changed form up to a boundary where it becomes thoroughly understood, and yet which is not carried beyond into the region of verbosity and tiresome and useless reiteration — is one of a high order, and it is one which Mr. Swett seems to possess to perfection. Its due and judicious exercise requires an accurate knowledge of the men whom it is employed upon, and the precise ideas and illustrations which are demanded by their comprehension. Mr. Swett has all these qualities, and the additional one of being an excellent logician and an admirable manager, who thus not only knows what should be presented, but the very best form in which the presentation should be made.

Possibly the not least remarkable feature of his oratorical power is found in his ability to employ pathos. Herein, when the occasion requires, he rises to a most effective level. He is both rhetorical and natural in this direction—the former being, to some extent, a sequence to the latter, in that he feels what he says, and therein, as usually happens, is eloquent. He is exceedingly happy in the use of this powerful element. When in this mood he smites the rock of men's hidden emotions, and obediently, as in the case of Moses, the waters gush forth in response to the summons. From the possession of this subtle power to touch effectively men's emotional natures, Mr. Swett has what the world would suspect from seeing him, and that is, a powerful element of poetry in his character. This is true; and its existence is not only the source of his power to touch the hearts of others, but it refines his nature, and gives him a chivalry that exhibits itself in a lofty regard for women, an integrity in business matters that can not be disturbed, and a kindly consideration that leavens all his intercourse with others. In fine, the poetical quality, while it introduces no element of effeminacy in his character, while it does not detract from his masculine vigor, or interfere with his comprehensive ability, softens his naturally rugged make-up, and gives him a needed and efficient refinement. In short, Mr. Swett is a gentleman who, as a lawyer, and more especially in the labor of conducting the trial of a case, occupies a very high and a very enviable position.

JOHN VAN ARMAN.

THIS gentleman was born in Plattsburgh, New York, in about 1818. He removed thence to Marshall, Michigan, and there began the practice of law. In 1859 he removed to Chicago.

He first obtained prominence some years ago in Michigan at the time of the notorious conspiracy against the Michigan Central railway. He was employed by the company to work up the case, and to assist in its prosecution. He went to work and got into the confidence of the leaders of the movement, joined the organization, shared in their councils and plans, and in this way possessed himself of all the secrets of the conspirators. At the time of trial, he assisted in the prosecution of the case, and alternated his duties in this direction by taking the stand as a witness for the State.

Since his residence in Chicago, Mr. Van Arman has taken a quite prominent position as a criminal lawyer. He is a man of very marked personal appearance, and of equally marked personal characteristics. He is of slender build, slightly round-shouldered, and of medium height. His head is small and narrow, indicating more force than comprehensive breadth. His eyes are small, black, glittering, and cunning in expression. His lower jaw is immense in breadth, and heavily armored with a convolute skin. His clean-shaven face is of a swarthy hue, which, with his small eyes, high cheek-bones, and stoical expression, gives him the appearance of an Indian parentage. His mouth is large, with heavy lips, and is occasionally parted in a smile which reveals rows of uneven teeth.

Mentally, he is *sui generis*. He is, perhaps, not an originator, but he seizes with instantaneous appreciation anything which may be found by others; and when he once closes upon anything, his bull-dog nature never lets it go. To speak in the style of the aborigines whom he so closely resembles, he can not often find a trail himself, but let it once be pointed out to him, and he will never lose it, or cease to follow it till the prey is overtaken.

It is doubtful that his veins run with warm blood. He is cold and passionless. His mental qualities may glisten, but it is not from the sheen of a flame, but from the reflection of icy surfaces. His intellect is clear, finely finished but frosty. His voice is dry and metallic, and his utterances before a jury are often venomous, always pointed and strong, but never warm or genial. Thawing the sympathies of a jury is something that he never attempted, nor would he know how to do it if he wished.

This glacial mechanism of his soul is never out of repair or working order. It has all the lubricity of ice, and moves powerfully, and without noise or friction. To these qualities he adds an industry in following up a case that never tires, that goes over a subject, no matter how vast, and omits no details, however numerous they may be or how microscopic. The law, the facts, the circumstances of a case, are each, in turn, made the subject of an examination that leaves nothing untouched, and hesitates at no labor or time which may be necessary to secure the investigation. He is a man that rarely laughs, and whose smile is not a smile, but a drawing back of the lips to show his teeth. He is a giant in industry, a Colossus in his patience, has indefatigable energy, is unrelenting in his stealthy and untiring pursuit of an enemy. Give him an end, and if patience, perseverance and industry can attain it, he will reach it; but it is a question as to his ability to provide a new plan in case his designed one be ruined. It is said by Judge Wilson that no man in Chicago is quicker than he to adapt himself to a sudden and unexpected change of circumstances. In any case, he is a very marked man — one whose great ability, coldness of nature, and success in his efforts, leave him with scarcely a rival.

With more warmth, more kindliness, he would take a high position in the world of legal and moral efforts.

JOHN N. JEWETT.

THIS gentleman was born in Maine. While very young, he removed to Wisconsin, but returned East, and graduated at Bowdoin College. He afterward came West again, and read law at Galena. In 1857 he removed to Chicago, and formed a partnership with Scates & McAllister.

Mr. Jewett is a gentleman of about forty-two years of age, although he looks five years younger. His hair is brown, and his beard the same. He is of medium height, slim, active, and well put together. He has keen, blue, very handsome eyes, and which are indicative, in many respects, of his character. His features are small, regular and attractive. His head is also small, but is filled with a brain of great activity. Intellectually, he is keen, sharp, quick.

As a lawyer, he is a general practitioner — is at home almost everywhere. He has himself always well in hand, and like a battery of light artillery, is always ready for attack or defense, or a change of position. His resources are always within reach. His mind is clear and incisive. While mild in conversation and oral argument, in writing he is pungent, severe and sarcastic, so much so that he has often reached the verge of toleration in his arguments before the Supreme Court. He is logical and strong, and his analytical powers are very great. His integrity is undoubted, and he is rigidly honest, not only with reference to himself, but his client and the opposing counsel. He is not rough or uncouth in his contact with others, with the exceptions above noted, but he has a manner which, while not being in the least effeminate, is almost womanly in its gentleness. His speeches are in keeping with his appearance — easy, fluent, graceful, deliberate and intellectual. He is ornate without being either florid or commonplace. What he has to say he says tersely, and in an attractive, forcible manner. As said, he is rather better in the office than before a jury, for the reason that he is painstaking, industrious and conscientious. Possibly there are few lawyers of his age who stand as well as he, or whose prospects are more promising. At present he is attorney for the Illinois Central Railway. He is also a member of the State Senate, the only public office he has ever filled.

H. G. MILLER.

MR. MILLER is about fifty-five years of age, and in personal appearance he is quite marked, and rather *distingué*, both in his appearance and demeanor. He is tall, well-proportioned, and very erect, with a somewhat stately bearing. His features are regular; his eyes blue, full and expressive; his forehead high and pyramidal; his hair gray, abundant, and thrown directly back. His mouth is small, and indicates a character of a good deal of resolution. The whole expression of his face is rather kindly, and withal dignified.

As a lawyer, he is very much respected by the profession. He is a man who, without being a profound legal scholar — albeit, a very excellent one — attains ends by his patient industry which men with a greater knowledge might fail to reach. His industry is one of the most important elements in his character, for the reason that by its aid he does many things which men more gifted by nature than himself do not often accomplish. He never reaches anything by flying to it, or by miraculous leaps. Whatever he attains he does by slow, patient, plodding, persistent effort. In some respects, he is an intellectual tortoise, who, like the one in the fable, not unfrequently reaches the goal far in advance of swifter-footed competitors. He is a man whose preparation of a case may be relied on as complete, thorough, exhaustive, providing it can be done by unremitting and pains-taking effort.

As a speaker, he makes no pretensions to a high order of elocution. He speaks more effectively to a judge than a jury. He has not a particle of imagination; and what is singular in this connection, is that in his speeches he sometimes essays the humorous. His grave mien, judicial deportment, slow-and-sure order of mental processes, form a combination from which one would suppose all ideas of the mirthful would be necessarily excluded. There is another inconsistency in his character, which this fact suggests. It is that, although patterned after the heavy artillery style, he is able to shift his position with considerable ease and speed, to meet an attack from an unexpected quarter. In meteorological parlance, he is weather-wise. He reads the skies which surround a case with great precision. He knows what a small cloud, or a change in the wind portends, and he is prompt in knowing what should be done to meet the forthcoming change. Heavy, and somewhat cumbersome in his mental operations, he yet possesses a surprising agility, when there occurs a sudden and pressing demand, for a shifting of position.

A faithful analysis of Mr. Miller's character necessitates the statement that he does well whatever he undertakes, but that he would have done just as well in in any other department of effort. Nature does not seem to have especially intended him for a lawyer. Had he been a wood-sawyer, he would have been just as patient, industrious, indefatigable, and gentlemanly in his manners as he now is. There are lawyers whom one could not imagine filling any other position, without their being out of place. In the case of Mr. Miller, it does not seem possible to imagine him in any position that he would not fill just as well as the one he now occupies. He would have made a stately and efficient President of a bank, or Superintendent of a railway, or diplomatist at some foreign court, or judge upon the bench, and in each instance he would have been just as stately and efficient as he is now in his position as a lawyer, and as a very respected and very estimable member of the bar of the Garden City.

VAN H. HIGGINS.

This gentlemen, one of the oldest and best known of the Chicago bar, is now about fifty years of age. He was born in Genesee county, New York. He came to Chicago in 1839, and was admitted to the bar in Iroquois county. He went to Galena in 1845, and practiced there with Judge Scott until 1853, when he removed to Chicago, and has always since been a resident. In the fall of 1858 he was sent to the Legislature, and the following spring he was elected Judge of the Superior Court. He served until the year 1863, when he resigned, and commenced the practice of law with Leonard Swett, his present partner.

In personal appearance, Mr. Higgins has a fine natural judicial presence. He is tall, well-formed, and of rather a commanding figure. His eyes are light-blue and deep-set, his complexion clear, and his forehead a regular three-story structure. His hair is tinged with gray, and his mouth is compressed and secretive. His entire face is sensitive, and yet it shadows forth indications of a character that may be iron-willed in case of necessity, and that may be or is, dogmatic and resolute under the majority of circumstances. In fine, this gentleman is one whom a stranger would regard as a man of fine appearance and great intelligence, while a muscular opponent would do no more than right if he hesitated somewhat before grappling with his erect, well-knit and stalwart frame.

The ability of Mr. Higgins as a lawyer, is not susceptible of a difference of opinion. Before he was Judge of the Superior Court his practice was one of the largest and most lucrative in the city. Since that time he has attended more or less to legal matters, but is not as active in his profession as he was before he went upon the bench, for the reason that he has very extended private interests of his own to attend to.

His head, which is that of a man of intellect, is additionally, in this direction, indicative of mechanical and mathematical tendencies. He is an inventor of no mean rank, and has several patents on original inventions or improvements. He is a fine theoretical as well as practical mechanician, and his judgment upon the merits of any new mechanical discovery is equal to that of the best practical mechanic in the West. Whether he is now the more lawyer or inventor is a nice question. It is certain, however, that his love for mechanical pursuits has grown almost to a mania; and that it absorbs a large share of his time, so that a biographical sketch of him would quite as properly belong to the Mechanics as the Lawyers of Chicago.

His style in the workshop is not pertinent to this article, although it would doubtless be of great interest. In his other capacity he is dignified, copious, and ponderous and incessant in his citations When he appears in court he carries always both arms full of law books, and has a porter who is heavily laden with the same material. His objections are frequent, and when arguing them he rises, and with his eyes fixed dreamily above the judge's head, he proceeds in a calm, self-possessed, unimpassioned manner to state his objections, and to present his authorities. He is an epitome of all the decisions that have ever been written, and what few he does not remember, he refers to readily, and reads *in extenso*. His quotations of authorities bearing on any point are only limited by one thing — the limits of the authorities themselves.

Judge Van Higgins is very generally respected, and is a man of fine intellect, great cultivation, and the possessor of many substantial qualities, both of heart and soul. The only doubt with the present writer is as to whether or not he should be classed as an inventor who is spoiling a good lawyer, or as a lawyer who is interfering with the progress of a superior inventor.

CHARLES CARROLL BONNEY.

THIS gentleman is a native of Hamilton, New York, one of the most beautiful places in the Chenango Valley, and widely known as the seat of Madison University. He spent his childhood on his father's farm on Bonney Hill, where his habits of thought were formed, and his ambition stimulated by meeting, among other visitors at his father's house, students from the University; and the prominent politicians, lawyers and divines of the locality.

When about seventeen years of age he commenced teaching, and began the study of the law. He continued to teach district and academic schools, and to pursue the study of his chosen profession until nearly ready for admission to the bar.

He removed to Illinois in 1850; located at Peoria; established an academic school called the Peoria Institute; was admitted to the bar at the age of twenty-one; commenced practice in the office of Judge Onslow Peters; and continued a successful general practice till 1860, when he removed to Chicago.

During his residence in Peoria the bar of Central Illinois, led by Purple and Manning, was one of the ablest in the West; and the practice thorough and exacting.

Since being a resident of Illinois, Mr. Bonney, until quite lately, has been very prominently before the State in some public capacity. In connection with Gov. French, Prof. Turner, Judge Skinner, and some other noted gentlemen, he was active and prominent in establishing the present educational system of Illinois. Since 1854 he has advocated a convention to secure uniformity of the statutes of the several States in relation to negotiable paper, conveyances, etc. He was one of the first to advocate in speeches and letters the constitutional prohibition of special legislation; and, some years before the war, procured the passage of resolutions in popular conventions in favor of a national currency, under a national law, in place of a wildcat system of State banks.

In 1857 he took a leading part in defeating the project of giving to a private corporation the control of the Illinois river; and he was engaged in some of the earlier cases on municipal subscriptions to railroads, taking the ground that they were unconstitutional. Since 1861 he has repeatedly advocated commissioners to represent the people, as to railroad and other private corporations, with summary judicial determination of questions concerning their respective rights and duties. It was he who first raised and argued the constitutionality of the excise tax on judicial process, and other State proceedings. He was also the first who stated the powers of the courts under the suspension of the *habeas corpus*, and presented the view which was reproduced two years later by Mr. Binney, of Philadelphia.

In his politics Mr. Bonney is a democrat, and he was very active in this direction, both as a speaker and a writer, until he left Peoria and removed to Chicago, since which he has given up all active participation in political matters.

As a lawyer Mr. Bonney has a wide reputation, his character as an advocate, and his legal writings, having frequently been the subject of favorable comment, in the public press of this, and of other States. He is a general practitioner, with a fondness for the specialties involved in inter-State law, and the legal relations connected with real estate, patents, and private corporations.

His preference seems to be for probate and equity business, rather than that of the common law, and it may be added that, though skilled in arts of pleading and practice, he is a lawyer whose tendency is toward settlement rather than litigation. He is an author of some note, having written and published a treatise on the Law of Railway Carriers; another on the Law of Marine, Fire and Life Insurance; and has works on several other subjects in course of preparation. He also edited, in a very finished and scholarly manner, the poetical works of the late Judge Arrington. His published addresses embrace orations on Freemasonry, and a variety of educational, political and legal subjects; and he is a frequent contributor to the public press of articles of a legal, financial, and literary nature.

Mr. Bonney's versatility is thus shown to be very great. A lover of his profession, he has acquired a competence by its practice, and has for it a devotion that finds its equal in the case of but few of the legal fraternity in the West. He is industrious in the extreme, and, although laboring hard as a lawyer, he yet finds time to cultivate literature, and to inform himself thoroughly concerning all the current questions of the day. In age he is about forty years, and in personal appearance he bears the marks of hard study, although he finds leisure to be courteous in his demeanor and affable in his conversation. His present associates are J. Edwards Fay and Charles W. Griggs, who occupy a leading position among the younger members of the Chicago bar.

In style Mr. Bonney is precise, incisive and clear, and withal a ready if not a redundant speaker, writer and conversationalist. His political speeches demonstrated the possession of an impassioned oratory, based upon a clear and comprehensive knowledge of the issues involved, and their germane facts. In the character of a politician, no speaker with whom he came in contact was more popular or more influential; and had he devoted himself to this department of effort, he might have attained almost anything within the gift of the people.

Mr. Bonney is a Swedenborgian in religion, is very active in his connection with Sabbath-schools, and has published a small pamphlet on the interpretation of the Bible. He is a Freemason of the rank of Knight Templar; and some years ago he received from the Masonic University of Kentucky the degree of Doctor of Laws.

He is domestic in his habits, and likes to gather about his fireside a congenial company for the elaboration of literary ideas, and the more graceful of the social qualities. A widely known and respected literary club is identified with his name; and he finds in literature a delightful recreation from the exhausting labors of professional life.

Although yet comparatively a young man he has already attained an enviable position as a lawyer, and author, and *litterateur*, and he has before him a future which promises still more flattering and enviable results.

CHARLES HITCHCOCK.

Mr. Hitchcock was born in Plymouth county, Massachusetts, in 1827, and is consequently now about forty-five years of age. He was educated in Hanover, New Hampshire, and graduated at that place in 1851. He took the law course at the Cambridge University, graduated in 1854, and came West, and has resided here, and devoted himself to the practice of his chosen profession, ever since. Within the time of his residence here, he has advanced himself to the front rank of the legal fraternity.

A stranger would scarcely take him to be a professional man. He is rather one who would be regarded as a moderate *bon vivant*, who has but little in life to trouble him, and who is in the enjoyment of an ample fortune. He is tall, has a large, portly figure, and is what would be termed an imposing, fine-looking gentleman. His face is not particularly indicative of intellect. His eyes are gray, and rather sleepy in expression, and his countenance promises latent rather than an active, belligerent energy. His hair and whiskers are gray, and his forehead receives additional height and expression from a slight premature baldness. Take him as he sits, and he seems a large kind of a locomotive, with powerful stroke and high driving-wheels, but with the steam low and the fire smoldering. One would conclude that all he needs to achieve great speed and vast power is firing up. There are men whose nervous temperament keeps them in perpetual motion, whether there is any demand for it or not. He, however, seems to be a sort of animal that has his seasons of hibernation, when he is torpid, and when he seems to be undergoing no other process than that of digesting his over-accumulated adipose matter.

As a lawyer, Mr. Hitchcock is among the best known and esteemed in the Northwest. His ability in this direction is not marked in any one direction at the expense of any other. He is not one of those men in whom some particular quality enlarges by feeding upon others. Thus it happens that, in mental character, social abilities and morals, he has undergone a remarkably even development. The same evenness is exhibited in his professional character,

He has, apparently, no specialty. He is equally good, and equally to be trusted, whether he be employed in chancery or admiralty, or as an advocate or a counsellor. He has, therefore, a very marked and unusual versatility, which seems to extend to every legitimate department of effort in his profession, and to a very thorough and even knowledge of men and things outside of it.

This universal evenness is disarranged somewhat in the surface of his professional character. While a very excellent advocate, he is not as good in this respect as he is as an attorney. His opinion in his office on the legal and other merits of a case is worth a certain number of dollars more than an address on the same matter before a jury. This is not because he is not a logical and thoroughly intelligent speaker, but it is because he is more of a logician than an orator. He argues well; but his argument lacks that divine fire which fuses the facts of a discourse irrevocably into the mind of a listener. He is not an unpleasant speaker. On the contrary, he is what is popularly known as a fine speaker. He has a clear voice, an imposing presence, and a graceful style. He, however, lacks imagination. He has no emotional development. He addresses the reason and never the feelings of a jury. He is cold and phlegmatic, and his speeches to a jury are like himself in this respect. He seems incapable of experiencing any of the more powerful emotions, and equally incapable of influencing in others these important elements in the human soul.

As the attorney needs no imagination, as its presence would be rather a hindrance and a nuisance than otherwise, the lack of it by Mr. Hitchcock makes him of more value when in the office than when before a jury. In his office, he is a very superior lawyer. His mind is very clear, active and accurate, and very pertinacious when he has once made up his conclusions. He is very methodical in his habits, and is remarkable for terse and clean-cut expressions — his papers always being in the fewest words, and always conveying the exact idea. Perhaps it may be said that his opinions on commercial law have no superior anywhere. He has a high notion of honor, and it is not probable that he would engage in an unjust cause, unless deceived by his client with reference to the facts. His opinion is of value, because it is based upon a very thorough knowledge of the law, and is reached by a singularly clear series of mental operations. He never becomes involved in obscurities. He is able to take a dozen apparently antagonistic authorities and reach the just conclusion without embarrassment or labor. He is not easily confused. He can reconcile conflicting situations and reach the desired end without difficulty. It is possible that, in taking a view of the bearings and merits of any case, he will primarily ascertain what is its technical character. After he has made up his mind as to what the authorities have to do with it, it may occur to him to examine its moral qualities. These, however, he would, as just said, subordinate to the legal value of any case. Not that he would lend himself to assist in the perpetration of any palpable wrong; but he is so much the more a lawyer than a moralist, that the first will naturally assert its precedence over the other.

It is thus seen that despite the assertion that he is very evenly balanced, he has some qualities that are subordinate to others. He is more of a lawyer than a moralist — in the sense above referred to; and a better attorney than an advocate, although he is both a high moralist and a fine advocate. Perfect balance in any character is fatal. Its result is to place the human mechanism in the condition of a wheel whose crank is " on a centre," and whose opposing forces are so alike that there can be no motion whatever. All great characters are a trifle off " the centre "; and hence, while Mr. Hitchcock is a superior conversationalist, advocate, attorney, chancery, real estate, and criminal lawyer, and a business man — although he is excellent in every one of these characters, he is, in some of them, better than in others; and thereby receives that mechanical preponderance in one direction or another which is essential to continuous motion.

Outside of his profession as well as in it, Mr. Hitchcock is greatly respected. He has fine social qualities, has an available fund of valuable general information, apart from his legal knowledge; and is believed to be the possessor of qualifications that would not be misplaced on the judicial bench. He was President of the late Constitutional Convention; and as such, his versatility came to his aid, and made him a dignified, able, and impartial officer.

Charles A. Dupee, a partner of Mr. Hitchcock, is a grave, quiet young man, of fine abilities, and fills a very important place in the firm of which he is a member.

SIDNEY SMITH.

THIS lawyer is one of the notabilities of the Chicago bar. He is noted as possessing very excellent ability, and also many personal peculiarities which render him what a scientific man would call, not the member of any species, but a "variety." He was born in New York, studied law with Church & Davis in the western part of the State, and was admitted to the bar in Albion, N. Y. He came to this city about fifteen years ago.

In personal appearance he is very marked. He is well and heavily built, and has in reality the physique of a prize-fighter. His face is regular and very swarthy. He has heavy, black hair, a thick, black moustache and piercing black eyes, whose upper lids, cut squarely across, add additional effect to their piercing character. His lower jaw is very heavy, and gives him a belligerent expression that is well supported by his pronounced chest, savage eyes, and shaggy hair. His voice is of the same noticeable character as the rest of him. As a lawyer he has some peculiarities, but he stands well. He has a high order of conscience, and does not regard one side of a suit just as good as the other. He is not apt to give his services in any case in which he thinks he will have to work against the interests of justice. He is very truthful and very bold, and one always knows just what he means simply by knowing what he says. He prepares a case with great care, and is very successful in cases whose decision turns on logic, evidence, preparation, management. Where there is anything emotional in a case he can not use it. In fine, in the preparation of a case he brings to bear upon it indefatigable industry, a comprehensive knowledge of the principles of law and of the authorities, and a logical appreciation of what is needed.

He tries a case a good deal with his external arrangements — his heavy jaw, his piercing eyes, and the elephantine roar of his voice. When he commences a suit he constitutes himself an Ishmaelite who looks upon all human kind as his enemy. This mannerism is the more singular and inexplicable in that Mr. Smith is at heart a very genial, kind-hearted gentleman, who has a thousand admirable qualities. But before a jury he is all muscle. Take him out of the courtroom, and he enjoys a good story in the hearing or telling as well as any man. Before a jury, the thing is too serious for anything like humor. He will laugh and be jolly when off a case, but once on it, he is on the war-path, and he brandishes his tomahawk and goes for scalps.

His speeches are logical, but sometimes so enveloped in thunder, and so barred with a network of ferocious gesticulations, that one is apt to lose sight of their real purpose in the stunned dismay with which he views their surroundings. Outside of the performance of his professional duties he is very popular among those who know him; but once in his war-paint, he is prepared and anxious to lift the hair of his best friend.

The legal profession has no more devoted lover of law than Mr. Smith. He is a man who hates shams, and who has no toleration for cant or humbug of any kind. He is as sincere in all his ways and beliefs as he is rugged, boisterous, and muscular in his developments before a jury. He is not a malicious man, for he has a trick of laughing with his eyes that is never seen save in one who is thoroughly good-natured and kindly at bottom. He has brains in abundance, and the judgment to use them effectively. What he needs more than anything else is toning down. He is keyed too high by several octaves. However, the abrading effects of time will wear off his rough edges. He is a diamond in the rough, and requires cutting and polishing. Time will doubtless accomplish these results, and then, in Mr. Smith, the bar of Chicago will have a finished diamond of the first water, for, despite all his personal peculiarities, he is universally recognized as one of the ablest and most successful lawyers in the profession in the Northwest.

WILLIAM H. KING.

Mr. King was born in Saratoga county, New York, about fifty years ago. He entered Union College, and graduated in 1846. He studied law under Hon. John K. Porter, of Waterford, and was admitted to the bar in 1847. He practiced law in Waterford till 1853, when he removed to Chicago, and has been a resident here since that time. He is now President of the Board of Education, and a member of the Illinois legislature.

Mr. King is a trifle below medium size, with keen black eyes, a good forehead, a pleasant, intellectual face, and a quick, energetic, nervous manner. His general appearance is suggestive of kindness, and of an active, restless character.

As a lawyer, Mr. King occupies a very excellent position. His practice is general, and his development very uniform. He is a good lawyer, whether in preparing a case, in trying it, or in presenting it either to a court or jury. He is a lawyer whose integrity is above all suspicion. He will only engage in just litigation, and once engaged he is on who gives the case a most thorough and conscientious treatment. He stands among the very first of those of his profession who may be relied on for indefatigable industry, pains-taking preparation and conduct of a case, unvarying courtesy towards everybody with whom they come in contact, and thorough and conscientious discharge of their duty to their client. These qualities has given him a excellent standing, and a lucrative and successful practice.

Apart from his profession, Mr. King is an affable, courteous gentleman. He has secured a competence from the practice of law, and he is sufficiently cultivated to permit him to enjoy life very thoroughly in his character as a private citizen.

Mr. George Payson, one of his partners, is a gentleman of about forty-five years of age, and is a son of the well-known Rev. Edward Payson. He is a very reliable lawyer in every department of legal practice, whether his duties be connected with the office or with the trial of a case in the courts.

The remaining partner, Ira Scott, is about forty-five years of age, is a student also of Hon. John K. Porter, is a very superior office lawyer, and a master in chancery.

M. F. TULEY.

THIS gentleman, now corporation counsel, is forty-four years of age, and was born in Louisville. He removed to Chicago in 1843, and studied law here, and attended the law school in Louisville in 1846. He was admitted to the bar in Chicago in 1847. During the Mexican war, he served three years in the volunteer service as First Lieutenant of Company F. of the Fifth Illinois Infantry. At the close of the war he went into New Mexico, and remained till 1854. During his residence there he filled the position of attorney general, and served two terms in the legislature. Since 1854 he has been practicing his profession in Chicago. He was elected to his present office in 1869.

Mr. Tuley is of medium size, with grey hair, blue eyes, and an older appearance than would be supposed from his age. He has seen very much of the world, and is a gentleman of considerable cultivation outside of his profession. He is very highly regarded, both as a gentleman and a lawyer. In his latter character, he is better in an office or in the conduct of a case than before a jury. He is not a fluent speaker, but he makes a very excellent argument before a judge, and in any instance in which the bare, logical presentation of facts are all that is demanded. In the preparation of a case he is very careful and pains-taking, and never presents anything until it has become all that laborious preparation can make it. As a manager he is very shrewd and cunning, much more so than would be supposed from his quiet face and demeanor, and more so even than is generally suspected by those who have long possessed his acquaintance.

WIRT DEXTER.

Mr. Dexter comes of a legal stock. His grandfather, his uncle, and his father were all distinguished members of the legal profession. In his celebrated speech against Hayne, Webster spoke of Samuel Dexter as "that great man of whom the gentleman has made honorable mention. He was a lawyer and he was also a statesman. A question of constitutional law was of all subjects that one which was best suited to his talents and learning. Aloof from technicality, and unfettered by artificial rule, such a question gave opportunity for that deep and clear analysis, that mighty grasp of principle, which so much distinguish his higher efforts. His very statement was argument; his inference seemed demonstration. The earnestness of his own conviction wrought conviction in others. One was convinced, and believed, and assented because it was gratifying, delightful, to think, and feel, and believe in unison with an intellect of such evident superiority." This gentleman was a member of John Adams' Cabinet, and was the grandfather of Mr. Dexter. His father Samuel, and his uncle Franklin Dexter, were lawyers of great prominence, so that Mr. Dexter is royally descended with respect to the legal standing of his ancestors. Mr. Dexter's father was a territorial judge in Michigan, after which he resumed the practice of law in the town of Dexter, which he founded. Wirt Dexter was born in that place, and always resided there until his removal to Chicago.

He is now about thirty-eight years of age, and hence his birth must have occurred about the year 1833. He went more or less to adjacent schools, and spent some little time at Ann Arbor, but left before obtaining his degree and entered an Eastern college. The other portions of his life before he came to Chicago were spent, in part, in the lumber regions, where he was engaged in reducing pine to the necessities of civilization, and in addressing his fellow citizens from the stump upon the political issues of the day. He is said to have been a young man whose maiden efforts at oratory were lofty and emphatic — a cross between the fervid pulpit efforts of a sincere Methodist preacher, and the gorgeous overflow of a young bird of freedom whose home is near the setting sun.

Mr. Dexter came to Chicago from Michigan about thirteen years ago, where, for awhile, he was engaged in the lumber business. He then commenced the study of law in the office of Sedgwick & Walker. In due time he was admitted to the bar, and within this period he has progressed from a raw youth from the lumber regions into one of the leading lawyers of the Northwest, and from — intellectually — nobody in particular, into one of the most influential and respected citizens of Chicago.

Mr. Dexter is tall, with a massive chest, and an athletic form which nothing less than the gymnastics of log-rolling could have developed. He has an open face, large, blue, expressive and kindly eyes, a high, broad forehead, and a full, dark-brown beard. His expression is one of refinement and intelligence, combined with a genial and dignified frankness. Taken in all respects, he is what most men would term a handsome man. With his grand torso, and long arms, he would have made a cavalry officer of most magnificent presence. But what the cavalry service has lost the legal profession has gained, for he stands in the very front rank of the latter.

As a lawyer he is both a superior advocate and a very excellent counsellor. In his latter character he is a student; and yet the student rather of general principles than of authorities. He has a very powerful intuitive ability to distinguish between right and wrong, and if he applies himself to the books it is for the purpose, not of ascertaining their conclusions, but of finding in them evidence to sustain the conclusions which his intuitions have already constructed. He seems to regard the law book as a means rather than an end; a something to be used as a witness to establish a certain case, and not as a judge whose decision is final.

This intuitive appreciation of what should be, without a slavish dependence upon authorities, is a fine and very excellent mental peculiarity. It is akin to an intelligent conscience; and a man who is guided by it will rarely — never knowingly — become involved in a wrong. This is the case with Mr. Dexter. It does not seem possible that he would take any case which he does not believe to be right. From the inspiration of these tuitions he has grown to abhor wrong, trickery, and even litigation itself, whose existence he believes unnecessary save as a very last resort.

As an advocate he stands well. His speeches always mean something, for they are always underlaid by the conviction that he is right. He always speaks with an earnestness which convinces a listener that he believes what he is saying. The tone of his speech is elevated, clear, and comprehensive. He occasionally introduces a humorous illustration, but never descends to buffoonry. Always it is evident that it is a gentleman who speaks. He talks with entire readiness, and is fond of interspersing his sentences with epigrammatic utterances from noted authors. His better efforts are classical in their purity, their clearness, and their sharp-cut outlines.

In his legal character, Mr. Dexter is influential for the reason that his firm is one of brains and cultivation, and because his personal influence in a case is of great weight. Men have confidence in him, because they know he will not advise them to commence a suit unless their cause is right, and that there is no remedy for them save litigation. It is a very strong indorsement that a man's case is perfectly just, and a substantial earnest that he will win it, when it is known that it is being carried by Mr. Dexter.

This gentleman has very fine social qualities. He is not of one idea, but converses easily and eloquently upon all ordinary topics. In his private life he is genial and affable, occupies a high social position, is luxurious in his habits, and artistic in his tastes and surroundings. He is liberal to the last degree, and his personal coöperation and that of his check-book may always be relied on in any case of public or private suffering. His generosity, intelligence, and geniality make him as much respected in private life, as he is in his professional character for his probity, dignity, eloquence and ability.

E. G. ASAY.

Mr. Asay was born in Philadelphia, and must be now somewhere in the vicinity of forty-five years of age. He enjoyed very good educational advantages in his youth, the which, with an enthusiastic disposition and a fine ability, he resolved to devote to the sacred calling of the ministry of the pulpit. He connected himself with the Methodist denomination, mainly, one who knows him would fancy, because it furnishes an outlet for a mercurial disposition and a springy, impetuous nature, such as is found in no other denomination.

He occupied himself for a time in the work of saving wandering sheep that were outside the fold, and in other pastoral duties, and was then taken from the pulpit and placed in the desk of a professor, at the head of an institution of learning connected with the Methodist church. How long he remained in this position, or why he concluded to change his profession, is not known to the writer; but it is known that, after a time, he transferred himself to the bar. From the pulpit to the bar is no great distance. The pastor who saves sinners from the damnation of sin, and the lawyer who saves criminals from the damnation of their offences, are not greatly removed from each other. These changes from the pulpit to the bar, and *vice versa*, are not uncommon. In fact, pulpit and bar are, in many respects, interchangeable terms; and he who practices in the Supreme Court established some eighteen hundred years ago, is not undergoing an ill-judged course of preparation for the mundane courts of chancery or of criminality.

Mr. Asay studied law in New York, and came to Chicago in 1856, since which time he has been actively engaged as a general practitioner, with a very decided tendency toward, and attachment for, criminal law and its practice. In respect to the latter branch of his profession, he has attained a first-class position. He has been prominent in many noted *causes célèbres* that have occurred in the West, among which the defense of Mollie Trussell, for the killing of the gambler Trussell, and the defense of the alleged conspirator, Charles Walsh, at Cincinnati, are best known to the public. His success in the practice of criminal law is proven by the fact that in Chicago he has had the charge of the defense of some forty capital cases, and in no instance have any of his clients ever suffered a capital conviction. In personal appearance, Mr. Asay is prepossessing, with the air of a cosmopolite. He is a little above medium height, with a massive, well-developed form. His head is broad, denoting a fine intellectual development; his eyes are a kindly blue, his lips full, and his countenance one expressive of great intelligence, geniality, and energy.

This quality of energy seems to pervade him most thoroughly. He is always wide-awake, and apparently driven. by a high-pressure, manifold horse-power mechanism. In conversation and in speech he dashes ahead with the *élan* of a French zouave in a *pas de charge*. He never appears to go *over* a subject — he goes *through* it, and sends obstructions flying in every direction, like a locomotive going at sixty miles an hour through a snow-drift.

He is an undoubted logician, but he forces convictions by his impetuosity. He does not so much reason things from his path, but he dashes them aside. Quick as a flash to catch a point, to detect a flaw, or avail himself of any sudden exigency, he is invaluable in the conduct of a case in which vigor, determination, and instantaneous comprehension of a character of a juror or witness are requisite qualities.

He is as genial in manner and conversation as can be desired. He is at home on all subjects; has an opinion on anything, or will have one, in a fraction of a second, on every topic that is presented ; he reads and analyzes character with a surprising readiness and accuracy; he has a large fund of fine humor, and is full of illustrations and reminiscences; he possesses an under-current of poetical ideas, that are always rising to and sparkling at the surface of his conversation; and he is a very general favorite with the bar and the public. In his private life he is noted for being fond of a luxurious domesticity, and as being a devoted bibliophilist, whose bibliolatry has brought together the finest and rarest private library in the West, if not on the continent.

THOMAS DENT.

MR. DENT was born in Putnam county, Illinois, November 14, 1831. At twelve years of age he became assistant, for a short time, in the Clerk's office of that county. He occasionally acted in that capacity during three years following, and acquired a taste for legal business and studies. At fifteen he was withdrawn from school to assist his father in the public offices of the county. In 1854 he was admitted to the bar, and was soon called to a full share of work in the county and upon the circuit. In the spring of 1856 he removed to Chicago and became associated in business with M. R. M. Wallace, now County Judge of Cook county. In 1857 he removed his office to Peoria, but he returned to Chicago the next year, and in the fall of 1860 entered into partnership with the late Judge Arrington, which association continued until the death of the latter. At present he is of the firm of Dent & Black.

In personal appearance Mr. Dent is delicate and feminine. His face is small and pale, with lines furrowing it in every direction, indicating severe study. His countenance is one that shows a very high order of intelligence. In his physical character there seems little of him. He is so slender that one almost feels a pity that one with so refined a face should be obliged to encounter the dangers of the streets without a guide and a protector in the person of a stalwart companion.

Physically, nature has done nothing for Mr. Dent. In an intellectual sense, what he is he has made himself. He is a student in the most comprehensive sense of the word. He looks as though he had neglected and exhausted his physical frame in building up his intellect. As a lawyer possessing a great knowledge of law, he stands very high. In his plodding, studious career, he has attended to a large number of cases in the Supreme Court of the State, and other courts of record, laboring assiduously in his calling, to which he is much attached. He presents a case always clearly and pointedly, and comprehensively, and when he has finished he has made every point that the case contains.

Socially, Mr. Dent's standing is very high. He is a prominent and influential member of the Third Presbyterian church, and is there, as in all his social relations, admired and respected. He has no enemies at the bar. They all admire his industry and respect his knowledge. Were he possessed of more physical energy, could his mental efforts be reinforced by a strong, vigorous frame, were he a trifle less a man of talent, and more a man of genius, he would take a very high rank. As it is, he stands well, and if patient, persevering industry can carry him to the front, he will surely, in time, attain that position.

MELVILLE W. FULLER.

MR. FULLER is a lawyer by descent as well as education. He is the son of a lawyer, and the grandson, on one side, of a lawyer, and on the other of Nathan Weston, at one time Chief Justice of the Supreme Court. He was born in Augusta, Maine, in 1833, and graduated, where all Maine men now graduate, at Bowdoin, in 1853. He commenced the study of law in Augusta, and finished in the Harvard law school. He was president of the common council of Augusta in 1856; and the same year left there and came to Chicago, where he has since resided. Since here he has taken quite a prominent position as a public man. He was a member of the Constitutional Convention in 1862, a democratic member of the Legislature in 1863, and a delegate to the National Democratic Convention in 1864. Although very devoted to his chosen profession, Mr. Fuller has always found time to be a democrat, and to do his share of the labors of the organization.

In person, he is a trifle less than medium height, with broad shoulders and a well-knit frame. He has a large, intellectual head, with intelligent gray eyes, a strong mouth, a luxurious moustache, and abundant hair slightly sprinkled with gray, and is a very good-looking gentleman, with a pleasant, intellectual face.

As a lawyer, Mr. Fuller has achieved a very high reputation from his legal services in general, and from the prominence with which he was brought before the public by his connection with the Whitehouse-Cheney case — an ecclesiastical proceeding whose details have become world-wide. In his profession he is a man of many resources, and is usually esteemed a manager whom it is no small labor to handle. He is very vigilant and active. He is a ready speaker, and has great fluency and speaks well. He is perhaps a better advocate than an attorney, for the reason that, in addition to his oratorical ability, there is more opportunity for adroit management in trying a case than in preparing it; nevertheless, he is industrious to the extreme, and he spares no pains, time or labor in bringing his cases to the very highest state of preparation. He is able to bring a very large amount of general learning into his speeches, and his use of the classics is at once extended and elegant. He is a bull-dog in pertinacity, never surrenders, and always pushes his cases to the last extremity. He gained notoriety as a lawyer in many important cases, and which involved great constitutional and political questions. Of late he has attracted attention in the Cheney case, and his oral argument before the Supreme Court in that case is regarded as of the very highest order.

His ambition, which is great politically as well as in his profession, spurs him into making the most of law and his ability. He is very cool in trying a case, and keeps his temper well, and therein has a great advantage over a more impetuous opponent. His tactics in such cases are good, for the reason that, whenever practicable, he never awaits to receive an attack, but always anticipates, by charging himself and putting the other party on the defensive. He is nervous without being timorous; and is very apt to indulge in flank or other movements in directions that are not watched by the opposing counsel. Perhaps the best evidence that he is devoted to the law is found in the fact that he continues its practice although sufficiently wealthy to live comfortably without it.

B. F. AYER.

THIS lawyer, the middle member of Beckwith, Ayer & Kales, was born in Rockingham county, New Hampshire, in 1825. He fitted himself for college at Albany, and graduated at Dartmouth in 1846. He studied law two years at Manchester, one year at Harvard, and was admitted to the bar in New Hampshire, in 1849. He practiced there until 1857, and was, during that time, Prosecuting Attorney for three years. He came to Chicago in 1857, and has since practiced law in this city. He was Corporation Counsel from 1861 to 1865, and filled the position most acceptably. At the present time, in addition to his other duties, he is the attorney for the South Park Commissioners.

As a lawyer, Mr. Ayer occupies a prominent position. He is better adapted for office business than for the trial of cases. He possesses very clear perceptions and great industry, so that he is not only entirely competent to go carefully through a case, but to reach with almost entire certainty, exact and correct conclusions. His integrity is as undoubted as his judgment is beyond dispute. He is regarded as very close, or, in other words, very exact and mathematical, in his mental processes. He has a very fine analytical mind, and has his ability in this direction so nicely adjusted that he can split a hair, with entire accuracy every time, "twixt south and southwest side." He is modest, reticent, undemonstrative, and unostentatious. As a speaker, he is easy, polished, fluent, forcible, but not imaginative.

Mr. Ayer looks much younger than his real age. He is of medium height, has a fine, intellectual head, blue eyes, regular features, abundant light hair, and a clean-shaved face. His looks indicate intelligence and refinement. He is a gentleman of cultivation outside of his profession, and is very much respected, both by his brother members of the bar and by the general public.

EMORY A. STORRS.

THIS well-known advocate was born in Cattaraugus county, New York, in 1834. He read law with his father and Marshall R. Champlain, now Attorney General of the State of New York. He was admitted to the bar in Buffalo, in 1855; and practiced law in New York city until 1859, when he came to Chicago.

Mr. Storrs is in many respects one of the most noted men at the Chicago bar. In thus having attained prominence, his shining qualities are not of an unmixed character. There is in him much to admire, and elements which would improve his character were they omitted. He has better qualities in abundance, and an ability which, if evenly developed, would place him at the very head of the legal profession in the West.

As a lawyer, Mr. Storrs has, as has been said, some qualities which have few equals and no superiors in the legal profession, either in Chicago or the country. As a jury lawyer, there is a domain in which he has no rival. His command of language is something marvelous; and his powers of ridicule and sarcasm, and his development of the humorous phases of any case, are unapproachable. He is, in these respects, brilliant and successful to an extreme. His comprehension and appreciation of the ludicrous are vast, and his ability to employ them is equally extensive. His efforts are always sparkling, intensely brilliant, and sometimes evanescent. What is strange in his oratorical character, is the fact that he is rarely pathetic. The man who has a keen appreciation of the humorous, rarely is unaccompanied by a corresponding susceptibility to its opposite. He who will laugh heartily will generally cry when due cause for tears is presented. If a jury whom Mr. Storrs addresses ever find themselves with their eyes filled with tears, is is from the fact of laughing over his funny presentation of some point, or his scoriation of some opposing lawyer or some unfortunate witness.

But these defects are the exception, possibly, rather than the rule in Mr. Storrs' forensic efforts. Many of his good things are born of the occasion, and this occasional spontaneity is a redeeming clause in Mr. Storrs' efforts as an advocate; and its results are often of a fineness, a pertinency, a superiority that indicate that their originator has in him many of the better qualities of the artist. In addition to these occasional risings above his commonplace and average efforts, Mr. Storrs possesses other excellent qualities. He is a hard student when necessity demands application, and he has not only the industry to work up a case, but the ability to comprehend it. He is willing to work, zealous in the cause of his client, and able to accomplish a good deal.

As a political speaker, Mr. Storrs has gained considerable position, and he, in this rôle, carries some weight. In this domain of effort, motives are not so much considered, and sincerity is not of so essential consequence.

In personal appearance, Mr. Storrs is below the medium height, is slender, with light hair and complexion, and blue eyes. He is quick in movement, and has a nervous style, that indicates an active organization. He has, in fine, many of the elements of a great man, and is a lawyer who is very successful, and who has more admirers and more haters than any other member of the profession in Chicago.

STEPHEN A. GOODWIN.

THIS well-known member of the Chicago bar was born in 1807, in Geneva, New York. He passed his extreme youth in Geneva, and in time removed with his father to Detroit. He entered Hamilton College in 1826, and passed from there to Union College in 1828, and graduated the following year. It may be mentioned in this connection that one of his classmates at Union College was Robert Toombs, between whom and young Goodwin there was no end of wordy war, Toombs being then an ardent champion of States' rights, and all the rest of the budget of extreme Southern views. He studied law with Hon. Geo. B., and E. T. Throop—afterwards Governor of New York —and was admitted to the bar at Auburn in 1831. Some time after this, he combined politics with law, taking an active interest in current political events. During the campaign accompanying Jackson's second nomination, he conducted a journal in the interest of Old Hickory, in which department of effort he succeeded not merely in distinguishing himself, but in doing excellent service for the party. For fifteen years prior to the abolition of Chancery practice in New York he was Clerk of the Seventh Circuit of the Chancery Court under the late Chancellor Walworth, and with which distinguished man he sustained extremely friendly and intimate relations.

During his practice of law in New York, the men with whom he was almost daily brought into professional contact, were Hon. Wm. H. Seward, Hon. Jno. C. Spencer, Hon. B. Davis Noxon, Hon. F. G. Jewett, Ex-Gov. Selden ; and from which contact he was necessarily obliged to develop his legal faculties with more than average rapidity and excellence.

In 1855 he removed to Detroit, and began the practice of his profession in that place, in company with his brother, who is now Judge of the Mackinaw Circuit. He remained there four years, and then removed to Chicago, in order to better accommodate the business which had grown up for him in this locality.

Mr. Goodwin is of marked personal appearance. He is quite tall, slender, erect, with dark complexion, high forehead, hair black, and slightly tinged with gray, regular features, and a countenance which is fine in detail, but ploughed with lines indicative of severe labor, and possibly somewhat care-worn and anxious in its expression.

There is, perhaps, no lawyer at the bar of the Northwest who has so varied an experience, and so extended a practice in every department of law, as Mr. Goodwin. In criminal, chancery, and admiralty practice, common law, and ecclesiastical matters, he has had a business which has extended over nearly half a century. At the present time he devotes himself mainly to patent law practice, and in this department he has achieved a very large success and constructed a business of great dimensions.

He is very evenly developed as a lawyer. Perhaps he is now more of a counsellor than an attorney, for the reason that his labors now mainly confine him to judicial, rather than jury arguments. Formerly, when his duties called him to lay a case before a jury, he was very highly successful, and had few superiors in this line of effort. He is a man of the greatest possible industry; and when once he has made the case of a client his own, he spares no effort to achieve success. His learning as a lawyer is profound and exhaustive; and in the matter of integrity, one more unimpeachable nowhere exists. His experience of men is varied almost beyond comprehension. He has studied them under every possible circumstance, having, while at Auburn, had a practice which extended not only over the entire State, but also over a great part of New England. Since leaving the East his territorial efforts have been quite as extended, and embrace operations in every State in the Northwest. In fine, it may be said that he is a gentleman who, professionally and socially, is thoroughly estimable, and this fact is recognized universally by those with whom he is thrown into contact.

ISAAC N. ARNOLD.

This gentleman, who has for many years occupied a prominent position before the public as a lawyer and politician, was born in Hartwick, Otsego County, New York, November 30, 1815. He had the customary educational advantages of the county schools and village academy, which he improved to such an extent as to give him a very fair preparation for the duties of practical life.

At the early age of fifteen he found himself thrown upon his own resources, and from that time began his struggle with the stern facts of existence, which served to strengthen and develop those mental and moral characteristics which have made him so much a man of influence and note. From seventeen to twenty he divided his time between academic study, teaching, and reading law, earning enough money by teaching half the year to enable him to pursue his studies the other half. He first entered the law office of Richard Cooper, of Cooperstown, N. Y., a nephew of the celebrated author, J. Fennimore Cooper, and subsequently became a student of Judge E. B. Morehouse. By assiduous application he soon acquired sufficient knowledge of law to make his services in the office available toward paying his expenses. In 1835 he was admitted to the Supreme Court of the State of New York, and immediately entered into partnership with Judge Morehouse, with whom he remained until he came West, in 1836.

In 1837 he entered into partnership with Mahlon D. Ogden, and afterwards became connected with E. C. Larned and Geo. W. Lay. During this year, Chicago having become an incorporated city, he was elected City Clerk, but his professional business increased so rapidly, that he resigned his Clerkship before the year expired, and confined himself exclusively to the practice of law. In 1842 he first took a prominent part in the politics of the State. At that time the question of State finances was the exciting topic. Public improvements, which were as yet unproductive of revenue, having brought the State deeply in debt, many prominent men were zealously advocating repudiation.

With the nice sense of honor for which Mr. Arnold has always been noted, he at once raised his voice in protest, and entered the field an active and efficient opponent of so questionable a proceeding. He was a delegate to the State Democratic Convention, and was also elected to the Legislature the same year, as the recognized champion of anti-repudiation.

In 1844 he was nominated as one of the Electors by the State Convention, and in 1848 was elected delegate to the Buffalo Convention, supporting with great earnestnes the Free Soil movement, and rendering substantial aid in organizing the new party, which had its birth at that time. In 1855 Mr. Arnold was again elected to the Legislature, and was the Free Soil candidate for Speaker, lacking only three or four votes of being elected. In 1858 he was an unsuccessful candidate for Congress before the Republican Convention of the then second district, John F. Farnsworth being his opponent. In 1860 he was elected to Congress over Mr. Farnsworth, by an overwhelming majority.

Up to this time, although taking an active part on the anti-slavery side of politics, in every campaign, State or National, Mr. Arnold had devoted himself assiduously to the practice of his profession, by which means he had won a leading place among the noted and successful lawyers of the West, having a professional income of $24,000 when he went into Congress. Retiring entirely from his profession, he gave himself up to his public duties, and for six years remained at Washington, expending each year $5,000 more than his compensation. In 1864 he declined a re-nomination to Congress, but received the appointment of Auditor of the Treasury for the Post-office Department, which position he resigned under Mr. Johnson's administration. Since that time Mr. Arnold has withdrawn from politics entirely, and devoted himself to the practice of his profession and literature.

He is a very excellent lawyer, very methodical in his habits, dignified before a Jury, and forcible and convincing when arguing before a Judge. He has made a specialty of criminal practice. His first important case of this kind was the trial of a negro named Dacit, in Otsego county, who was accused of murdering his brother. Mr. Arnold being satisfied of his innocence, volunteered to defend him, and procured his acquittal. This was the beginning of an extensive criminal practice, during which no man defended by him was ever convicted. Among other noted causes in which he has appeared as counsel, that of Taylor Driscoll, charged with the murder of John Campbell, the leader of a band of "regulators," in Ogle county, is perhaps the most celebrated ; while the cases of Henry Bridenbecke, and German, both charged with murder, in McHenry county, and of Green, in this city, are of equal interest.

Mr. Arnold has a keen, analytical mind, is a close observer, and, without possessing genius, possesses so much talent that it is difficult to draw the line. He is wiry, shrewd and untiring, a deep thinker, and a speaker of fluency and ability.

As an author Mr. Arnold has also achieved signal success. His "Life of Lincoln" is generally conceded to be the most complete and faithful record of that great man's career, and of the history of the overthrow of slavery ever given to the public. His close and intimate relations with Mr. Lincoln gave him advantages which, with his appreciative admiration of his subject, combined with a facile pen, enabled him to give with accuracy, as well as elegance of diction, the history of the most interesting and exciting times of our late war.

In personal appearance Mr. Arnold is tall, slender, and stately. He has a high, prominent forehead, thin grey hair, an aquiline nose, keen, grey eyes under heavy brows, a thin, closely shut mouth, and a full beard, well trimmed and grey. In manner he is courtly, affable and rather elaborate, after the manner of the old règime, and always looks and acts the polished, courteous gentleman.

GEORGE C. BATES.

THIS Nestor of the Western bar is a native of Canandaigua, New York, and was born in 1814. He studied law in the office of Hon. John C. Spencer, reading with him three years. In 1834 he went to Detroit, and was there admitted to the bar. He soon obtained a large collecting practice, which extended to Indiana and Northern Illinois. In 1841, he was appointed United States District Attorney by General Harrison, but resigned at Harrison's death. He was re-appointed to the same position by Taylor; and he held the office until 1852, when he resigned and went to California, and there filled the position of assistant counsel in government cases. Five years later, he returned to Detroit, having accumulated a large fortune during his California career. In 1861 he came to Chicago, and since that time he has been in general practice. He was admitted to the bar cotemporaneously with Hon. Thomas Hoyne and the late Judge George Manierre, of this city, and is, therefore, one of the oldest members of the bar in the West. While his line of practice is general, he has had a good deal to do with revenue and admiralty matters, for which he is eminently fitted from his long connection with official positions.

Mr. Bates is of medium size, with gray hair and moustache, keen, handsome dark eyes, and a pleasing, intelligent face. He has been very prominently identified with political matters, and as a speaker has been in very constant demand. He is an advocate rather than an office lawyer, and as such he has achieved a very marked success. He is a gentleman of the old school, very affable and courteous, is the possessor of a very large amount of genuine *esprit de corps*, and, it may be added, is very generally respected by those who know him.

IRA O. WILKINSON.

HON. IRA O. WILKINSON was born in Virginia, and is about fifty years of age. In 1835 he became a resident of Jacksonville, Illinois, where he was educated and studied law with Judge William Thomas. On being admitted to the bar he formed a copartnership with Hon. Richard Yates, which was relinquished when he removed to Rock Island in 1845. Here he built up an extensive and successful practice, and was elected and served for two terms as Judge of the Sixth Judicial District, in which position he obtained an enviable record and gave very general satisfaction. In 1867 he removed to Chicago, and is now the senior partner of the firm of Wilkinson, Sackett & Bean.

Judge Wilkinson is unassuming in his manners, dignified and courteous in his deportment, and, without the circle of his intimate friends, somewhat inclined to reticence. He has a vigorous and well-balanced mind, trained and developed by liberal professional and general culture. He possesses undoubted integrity, and in his practice unites the probity and fairness of the judge with the acumen and fidelity of the lawyer. He is thoroughly familiar with the general principles of the law, and in argument he reasons from his own premises, deduces his own conclusions, and uses cases only so far as they illustrate principles. He is a counselor rather than an advocate, and, as such, is a very safe adviser.

ISRAEL N. STILES.

GENERAL STILES was born in 1833, in Suffield, Connecticut, on a farm, where he remained till sixteen years of age, working in summer and attending the district school in winter. At the age of nineteen he removed to Lafayette, Indiana, and commenced reading in a law-office, having read law the year before coming West. Soon after he took a school a few miles out of town. At night he taught singing school, and the while carried on his law studies. The next year he opened a private school, and continued reading law until 1855, when he was admitted to the bar. About this time, Lawrence, in Kansas, was burned, and at a public meeting, young Stiles developed an oratorical ability that astonished every one. Thereafter he rose rapidly into prominence. During the Fremont-Buchanan campaign he made sixty-six regular speeches through the country, one of which was given in Music Hall, Boston, and another in Augusta, Maine. He was prosecuting attorney for two years, and subsequently was elected to the State Legislature.

He was beginning to get ahead in law practice when the war broke out. He raised a company, although married the same month. Somebody else received the captaincy of his company, and then he enlisted as a private, but was made Adjutant to the 20th Indiana. He was captured at Malvern Hill, and was in Libby six weeks, and was then exchanged. He was made Major of the 63d Indiana, then Lieutenant-Colonel of the same regiment, and finally Brigadier General, his commission dating from the battle of Franklin, Tennessee. After the war he came to Chicago, and practised law alone until he entered into partnership with Judge McAllister, in 1867. Two years later he was elected City Attorney, which position he now holds.

This sketch of the life of General Stiles has been made thus extended, because its incidents prove better than any mere assertion, his extraordinary versatility, and the energy of a character by whose aid he has raised himself from obscurity to his present position.

As a lawyer he is rather more of an advocate than an attorney, and it may safely be added that, in the trial of cases he has few superiors at the bar of Chicago. He is very adroit in the management of a case, and has a power and a quickness of repartee, and an ability to avail himself of emergencies that are singularly effective in his clients' interests, and uncomfortable for the plans of opposing counsel. Whenever he presents a case to the court, he is always prepared with the authorities which support the legal propositions involved, and in this particular he is usually clear and complete in his preparation. As an advocate he has much ability. He always seems sincere, and wields a most effective, pathetic power; and as a public speaker, one who is ready, fluent and logical, and who can tell an apt story with incomparable mimetic power, he has few or no equals of his age in the Northwest. As he is yet a comparatively young man, he has before him a future of great promise.

In appearance he is slender, of medium height, rather swarthy in complexion, with keen, full, dark eyes, and dark beard worn full. Socially he is much liked. He converses well on all general subjects, and has just a flavor of satire in his conversation sufficient to render it palatable. He is profuse in his illustrations, possesses a fine fund of anecdote and humor, which renders intercourse with him a matter of great social and intellectual enjoyment; and as a post-prandial orator he is happy, humorous, and effective far beyond the average in this class of efforts. With reference to his course as City Attorney, his success may be best comprehended from the character of a remark, made a few days since in court, by an eminent lawyer who was opposing him in a city case, and who warned the jury that his apparent fairness in arguing a case, and which was calculated to mislead them, had saved the city, since he had become City Attorney, thousands of dollars.

CHARLES H. REED.

Mr. REED was born in Strykersville, Wyoming county, New York, in 1834. He attended school and worked on a farm during his younger days; and later, taught school, and attended an academy until he entered Yale College. He studied law, and was admitted to the bar in 1858, in Henry county, in Illinois. He removed from that place to Rock Island, and, in 1860, in company with Hon. Joseph Knox, he removed to Chicago. He practiced law till 1864, when he was elected District Attorney, an office which he still holds.

Mr. Reed is tall, broad-shouldered, well-formed, with light hair, moustache and imperial, regular and intelligent features, and blue eyes. In his movements he is quick, nervous, and therein indicates his character. He is a well-read lawyer, has a great deal of positive character, and is a very shrewd manager. He possesses as much influence as any man in Chicago; employs a vast amount of energy; and pushes everything forward with resistless force. In his character as a public prosecutor, he has shown himself the possessor of great industry, and the ability to dispose of a vast quantity of work within a very short time. In this direction, he is indefatigable and industrious; and the result is that he is universally acknowledged to be a thorough, efficient, and economical official.

Notwithstanding the immense amount of labor which his official position, in addition to his private business, entails upon him, he finds leisure to devote to study; and in addition to his attainments as a lawyer, he is one of the finest classic scholars in the northwest. His translations from the Greek have won him an enviable reputation as a close student, while his contributions to general literature stamp him as a writer of undoubted merit.

Socially he is very genial, and is very much liked by all who know him; and he is at once a capable, intelligent and industrious public officer, and a popular, much-esteemed gentleman.

WILLIAM B. SNOWHOOK.

THIS well-known gentleman was born in Ireland, in 1817, and came to New York without the aid of relatives or friends, when but eight years of age. His life from that time has been a very eventful one in many respects. He early commenced reading law, but all the time carried on some other business. He was a contractor while in the East, and later, was the same in connection with William B. Ogden and others on the Lake Michigan canal. He has been in the commission business, and various other pursuits, but always kept up his legal studies. He was Collector of Customs under Polk and Pierce, and has also held other public offices of trust and consequence. In 1857 he was admitted to the bar, after which he spent two years in the law department of the Chicago University, and graduated with honor.

It is gratifying to be able to state that all this persistence has had its reward. Mr. Snowhook is now not only a very able and respected lawyer, but a very successful one. He has obtained a very good scholastic education, in addition to his legal one; and by his energy has secured a very handsome competence. He is a very hard worker, coming to his office at six in the summer and seven in the winter, and his habit is to devote himself to his business until night without intermission. As an example of what energy, determination and perseverance can accomplish, Mr. Snowhook stands, at the Chicago bar, with scarcely a rival.

LAMBERT TREE.

MR. TREE is a graduate of Columbia College, in Washington. He studied law with James Carlyle, who is now a leading practitioner before the Supreme Court at the national capital. He read law two years, and then graduated at the University of Virginia, in the law department. He came to Chicago in 1855, and in time became a member of the firm of Tree & Clarkson.

Mr. Tree is a very affable and scholarly member of the legal profession. He has fine abilities, and, prior to his late visits to Europe, he was a close student and a ready practitioner. He is in the possession of a very ample fortune, and his time is much occupied by the management of his private interests, but nevertheless he gives his attention to office business, and in this direction is very constantly engaged. He goes into court but little, and has a large business in the line of real estate practice, and the management of the legal affairs of several heavy corporations. He is an easy, fluent conversationalist, a gentleman of fine general cultivation, and a very respected citizen. Were he thrown on his own resources, and obliged to make his way in life by his own abilities, he would achieve a decided success in the legal or any other department of effort.

D. L. SHOREY.

THIS gentleman takes a very excellent rank as a lawyer, and he is a man who is very much respected and trusted by those who know him. He is a native of Maine, graduated in the class of 1851 at Dartmouth College, and came West in 1855. He studied law at Cambridge, and was admitted to the bar in Boston, in 1854. He removed to Chicago in 1865. For three years, while in Davenport, Iowa, he was City Attorney, which is the only office he has ever held, although since being here he has been spoken of in connection with a judicial position. He prepares and tries his own cases, is a lawyer of a high order of character, and has established a fine reputation since his short residence in Chicago. He is regarded as a very able man; is very quiet, and has very high judicial abilities.

JOSEPH B. LEAKE.

MR. LEAKE is essentially a Western man, although of Eastern birth, having been a resident of various Western States since eight years of age. He was born in Cumberland county, New Jersey, on the 1st day of April, 1828. In 1836 the family removed to Cincinnati, and from that time Mr. Leake has been identified with the West.

He received his preparatory education in the schools of Cincinnati; graduated at Miami College, Oxford, Ohio, in the class of 1846; studied law in the office of Groesbeck & Telford, of Cincinnati; was admitted to the bar of the Supreme Court of Ohio January 16, 1850; and practiced law in Cincinnati until 1856. Induced by failing health to seek a change of climate, he removed to Davenport, Iowa, and opened an office, devoting himself with great assiduity to building up a lucrative business. At the special war session in May, 1861, he was elected to the House of Representatives, and the same fall was elected member of the Senate. He served through the session commencing January, 1862, and at the close was elected President of the Senate *pro tem*.

At the second call of the President in the summer of 1862 for more men, Mr. Leake resigned his seat in the Senate, recruited a company, of which he was elected Captain, and mustered into the 20th Iowa Infantry. He was immediately afterward commissioned Lieutenant-Colonel, and as such commanded the regiment until the close of the war, serving in the Army of the frontier at Vicksburg, and then with the Army of the Gulf until the capture of Mobile. Mr. Leake's war record is a good one, he having been breveted Brigadier-General of volunteers for bravery on the field. In July, 1865, he was mustered out of service, and returned to his home in Davenport. He had no sooner removed his uniform than he was again in the office, and was ready to resume professional business. At the general election held the same fall, he was again sent to the Senate, and served through the session, commencing January, 1866, as Chairman of the Judiciary Committee. In 1867, the lawyer getting the ascendancy over the politician, Mr. Leake resigned his seat in the

Senate and retired to private life, devoting himself, with a good deal of quiet energy, to the law, which in return gave him a large and remunerative practice. He was elected attorney for the county, and served in that capacity until his removal to Chicago in November, 1871.

As a lawyer Mr. Leake occupies a good position, both as a counselor and an advocate. His opinions are reliable and his judgment correct. He is well read, and devotes himself entirely to his profession. As yet he has developed no specialty in practice, but does a general business, and is considered equally good in any branch of the law. In personal appearance, Mr. Leake is a tall, well-built, handsome blond, still young, and looking younger than figures would indicate to be his age. He is quiet, unobtrusive and courteous in manner, and is equally at home in the *role* of lawyer or dispensing the general amenities of social life.

GRANT GOODRICH.

The subject of this sketch is the youngest of twelve children, and was born in Milton, Saratoga county, New York, August 7, 1812. When four years old, his father moved to Chautauqua county, purchased a large tract of land and settled upon it. Being a man of great energy and spirit, and especially active in the promotion of education, he had a school taught in his own house two winters, which, with his own and a few of the neighbors' children, had a very respectable roll-call.

Until fifteen he attended the county schools, when symptoms of consumption — a hereditary disease — showing themselves, he abandoned school and went on to the lakes. He had since boyhood been enamored with the ideal sailor's life, but this little experience in the actual duties of a seaman not only cured his lungs but his relish for the water, and he returned from his trip converted to a full belief in the substantial superiority of land over water.

He immediately, upon his return, entered the academy at Westfield, and remained two years and a half; then went into the law office of Dixon & Smith, staying with them until he came to Chicago, in 1834.

He first entered into partnership with A. N. Fullerton, but at the expiration of a year dissolved it, and formed a copartnership with Judge Spring, which continued until shortly previous to his election as Judge. In the crash of 1837 Mr. Goodrich was heavily involved, but by hard work and an invincible honesty these obligations were met, and not only principal but interest were paid. He was very successful professionally, and until 1857 his practice grew constantly larger and more profitable; but in 1858 he was obliged to relinquish it and go abroad to recuperate, the severe labors of the preceding years having told heavily on his health.

As a lawyer and Judge, Mr. Goodrich's reputation is unsurpassed. He is positive, radical and unflinching in everything he undertakes, and if success be secured by energy, determination and hard work, it it is a foregone conclusion.

At present he devotes himself to office business mainly, retiring on his well earned laurels and wealth to an easier life.

He is an earnest Methodist, and attends to spiritual matters with the same earnestness and energy that have characterized his treatment of temporal things. In fine, he is a good lawyer, a just Judge, a genial gentleman, and being wealthy, enjoys himself without allowing anything to greatly trouble him.

E. B. SHERMAN.

MR. SHERMAN is a native of Vermont, passed his early years upon a farm. Graduated in 1860 at Middlebury College with honors, and subsequently from the Chicago Law University. He engaged for a time in teaching, in which he became distinguished, and was in the army during the war. He is a hard worker, a gentlemen of a very high order of attainments, and a finished scholar. Thoroughly honest and reliable, and entering with great energy and enthusiasm upon whatever he undertakes, he has built up a large practice, and is rising rapidly in the profession. He is well known as a public speaker in many parts of the State, has had some experience in journalism, and perhaps fine oratorical and literary abilities. Immediately after the great fire, he was selected by the Grand Lodge of Odd Fellows as a member of the Relief Committee, and as its Secretary he performed an immense amount of labor, discharging the difficult and perplexing duties of the position with eminent ability, and received therefor the most flattering commendations of the highest officers of that fraternity.

BENJAMIN D. MAGRUDER.

THIS gentleman is a native of Mississippi, having been born near Natchez, but in Jefferson County, Sept. 27, 1838. His early boyhood was spent on his father's plantation, which had been in the family since the early part of the present century. His father, W. H. N. Magruder, a graduate of the Wesleyan University, of Middletown, Connecticut, and college professor, was his preceptor, and prepared him for college at the early age of fourteen, at which time he went to New Haven, Connecticut, and entered Yale College. He was graduated in the class of 1856, and immediately after returned to his Southern home. His father in the meantime had opened a private collegiate institute at Baton Rouge, and the three years following were spent in teaching, and studying law. The last year, Mr. Magruder attended the Law School of the University of Louisiana at New Orleans, and graduated, valedictorian, in 1859. In August of the same year, he went to Memphis, Tennessee. and opened a law office, having barely attained his majority. His extreme youthfulness, which had not prevented his passing a brilliant examination, was responsible for a tardy practice, and in 1860, he aceepted a situation in the office of Master of Chancery, which position he occupied till the war broke out in 1861. Fifteen days after the fall of Sumpter he left Memphis and went to New Haven, Conn., where, in the home of his grandfather, Rev. Dr. Heman Bangs, he found a warm welcome. This course was most seriously criticised by his Southern friends, but the principles, imbibed from old Yale and his New England grandparents, and his convictions of right, were stronger than ties of blood or partisan feeling, and Mr. Magruder, with the conscientiousness which is so characteristic of the man, maintained his loyalty to his country, and came North.

In June, 1861, he came to Chicago, commenced the practice of law, and since that time has devoted himself entirely to his profession. During the war, when sectional feeling ran so high, Mr. Magruder, whose political convictions were radical in the extreme, but who was bound by ties of blood to the South, could not bring himself to take up arms against them, and, therefore, avoided all political notice and discussion, and confined himself exclusively to business. Upon the death of Judge William Mather in 1868, he was appointed his successor as Master of Chancery, which office he now holds, and in addition to the onerous duties of the office, attends to a large and constantly increasing practice.

Mr. Magruder is still a very young man, but with the position he has already achieved, and the more than ordinary ability he possesses, there is not a fairer prospect before any member of the profession. He is a very acute reasoner, and a diligent student, and especially happy in the selection of facts and cases which illustrate a point or prove a precedent.

Mr. Magruder's personal appearance is pleasing, and his manner polished and courteous. He has the jetty hair and beard, piercing black eye, and colorless olive skin which we associate with warm climates; and he has also the quick temper, the genial hospitality and open generosity which characterizes the well bred Southerner.

GEORGE HERBERT.

HE is a native of Maine, and is about fifty years of age. He comes of a legal family, which reaches back through several generations, while his father was one of the most prominent lawyers of his native State. He graduated at Amherst, and soon after commenced the practice of law, and at once took a leading position in the profession. About twenty years ago he came to Chicago. For a time, he engaged in the lumber business, but of late years has devoted himself exclusively to law practice. He is a thoroughly well-read lawyer, and possesses eminently a legal mind, which comprehends legal principles, as it were, by intuition, and is quick to apply them to the case in point. He is very prominent and influential in the Congregational Church, and a gentleman who has superior cultivation and very fine social qualities.

HENRY S. MONROE.

THIS gentleman was born in Baltimore, and is now about forty years of age. He read law in the office of the well-known Henry R. Mygatt, at Oxford, in Chenango county, New York. He was admitted to the bar at that place in 1854, and immediately after removed to Chicago, and has, since that time, been a resident of this city, and has devoted himself wholly to the practice of his profession.

Mr. Monroe is one of our best-known and most popular citizens. He is very affable in his manners, is a bibliopholist of some considerable note, and occupies a very superior position as a lawyer. In this respect he has achieved a very decided success, and has succeeded in acquiring a very handsome fortune by his industry in his profession. He has devoted himself very largely to real estate law; and herein has proved himself not only thoroughly reliable, of excellent judgment, but a manager of no second-rate ability. He is very shrewd, far-seeing and calculating; a man of wondrous industry, knows what legal principles are applicable to the case in hand, prepares all his cases with the utmost care, and knows what external influences are to be met, controlled or conciliated. He has risen to his present position solely by his own energy; and now that he has secured it, he holds it easily, and makes the most of his surroundings. He is as good a judge of a horse as of a piece of real estate, which is paying his knowledge of the former the highest possible compliment. In fine, he is an excellent lawyer, a very popular gentleman, and a man of fine tastes, and given to the pursuit of rational enjoyments.

EDWARD ROBY.

THIS gentleman was born in Brockport, N. Y., in 1840. In 1857 he entered an office in Lockport, N. Y., and applied himself closely to the study of the law, and in 1861 was admitted to the bar in Albany, N. Y. In 1862, his health failed, accompanied by a serious affection of the eyes, which necessitated an entire withdrawal from study. He left the office and went to the oil regions, where he engaged in manufactures and other general business until 1865, when he again commenced his professional work, came to Chicago, and opened an office.

Like all large cities, Chicago was full of struggling young lawyers, who were to rise or fall as their own ability should determine; but Mr. Roby, undaunted by the unsuccessful numbers who had come and gone, remained, determined to succeed, and succeed in Chicago. He possessed none of the dash which pushes a man into sudden notoriety or success, and three years passed without his having gained more than ordinary success. During this time he had speculated some in real estate. By this means his attention was first called to the loose and, as he believed, illegal way in which the revenue laws were administered. He applied himself to the study of the law pertaining to the subject, and mastered every detail, deciding that here was a field of action which could be successfully worked. In 1868 he was retained as counsel in his first tax suit, and in the fall of the same year won his first case in the Supreme Court of Illinois. The next year he had twenty-one cases, the following year eighty-three, and in 1871 one hundred and seventeen, all of which were carried through successfully, with the exception of fifteen. Among the most noted of these was that of Rich *vs.* Chicago, which became the leading case on special assessments and eminent domain, reversing, on constitutional grounds, all the special assessment cases found in the ordinary records, with four or five exceptions.

As a lawyer, he is considered well read, competent and industrious; an opponent, who, if patience, persistence and hard work will win a case, is hard to beat. He makes no pretensions as a speaker;

in fact, never makes an argument before a jury, but in any matter which requires minute investigation, exact knowledge of the law and authorities, unwearied industry, and a pertinacity which never yields a point without strenuous resistance, he is, perhaps, without a rival.

In personal appearance Mr. Roby looks more like a college professor or *literateur* than the wiry, hard-working lawyer. He is of medium height and slender build. His face is thin, an incipient baldness giving an appearance of additional height to the forehead and a long look to the face. Keen, small, dark eyes restlessly take observations on everything passing. A projecting chin and square jaw give an expression of force and character to a face otherwise almost feminine in its delicacy.

His mental qualities are as marked as his features. He is a close observer, an indefatigable worker, keen, cool and persistant; a man who will not stay beaten until every court in the land has given his case a hearing. He drives a good pair of horses, but gives little time to social enjoyments, devoting himself to the particular lines of his profession of which he has made a specialty, and in which he has achieved very substantial success.

JAMES B. BRADWELL.

THIS gentleman was born in England in 1828, and came to this country when but sixteen months old. He removed to Illinois in 1834, and has been in the West and South since that time. He began the study of law in Memphis, and was admitted to the bar in Chicago in 1853. He is a tall, fine-looking gentleman, with dark eyes, beard and hair. He is widely known for his progressive views on some of the prominent questions of the day, and is thoroughly liked and respected by those who know him.

He served as Probate Judge for eight years, and while in this position he collected a library of probate law that is second to but one or two in this country. In his knowledge of probate law especially, he has no superior in this place or any other, and his moral courage, like his thorough honesty, is of the very highest order.

EVARTS VAN BUREN.

JUDGE Van Buren was born in Kinderhook, New York, in 1803. He was admitted to the bar in 1827, when he removed to Penn Yan, where he was thrown among some of the best legal and political men of the day. In 1836 he removed to Buffalo; in 1840 he went back to Penn Yan; in 1856 he came to Chicago, and in 1861 he was elected Judge of the Recorder's Court. After serving one term, he resumed the practice of law, in which he is now engaged. He is one of our oldest and best known practitioners, and has passed an eventful life, in which he has taken a prominent part in politics, and in some criminal suits, which, at the time of their occurrence, attained a world-wide notoriety. In his private life he is a very genial gentleman, and as such he is very much liked by those who have his acquaintance.

JOSEPH P. CLARKSON.

THIS lawyer is a graduate of St. James College, Maryland, and studied law in Hagarstown, in the same State. He came to Chicago in 1851, and was admitted to the bar, and then entered into partnership with Buckner S. Morris. After a while Robert Hervey was added to the firm, and it thus remained until Judge Morris went on the bench. At the present time, Mr. Clarkson is the senior member of the firm of Clarkson & Van Schaack.

Mr. Clarkson is a gentleman about fifty years of age, with a countenance indicative of great energy and intelligence. He is a very capable and excellent lawyer, who prepares a case with extreme fidelity, regardless of the amount of labor involved or the time to be consumed. He also tries it carefully and thoroughly, and although effective before a jury, his chief excellence lies in the direction of a legal argument before a court. He is the only lawyer in Chicago who has ever done anything in the line of dramatic and trade-mark copyright cases. He has handled several very important ones that have occurred in Chicago courts, and, it may be added, in each case with entire success. In fine, he is a gentleman, who, in his professional and private life is entitled to, and who receives a very general and very cordial support.

ELLIOT ANTHONY.

THIS lawyer is an author of some note, and a gentleman of very considerable ability in many respects. He has industry, and will work up everything there may be in a case. He spares nothing in this direction, and can be relied on for perseverance, and a conscientious performance of whatever he may have to do. He leaves nothing unfinished. His preparation of the complicated details growing from a litigation to prevent the consolidation of the Galena and Northwestern railroads is a marvel in its completeness and elaboration, and as such has received recognition by the entire bar of the country.

E. F. RUNYAN.

THIS gentleman is probably one of the most active citizens of Chicago, and one of the most busy men in the legal profession, in which character he probably tries more cases than any other lawyer in Chicago. As a lawyer he has a great amount of shrewdness, and is excellently well posted on rules of practice. He is about forty years of age, is nervous, angular, and always tremendously occupied. He is a member of the Board of Education, and of several other boards, and of almost everything else of a public character in Chicago; and he finds time to attend to them all, and to adequately care for the duties of his profession.

JOHN LYLE KING.

MR. KING was born in Madison, Indiana, in 1823; and he resided there until 1856. He was admitted to the bar in 1847 by the Supreme Court of Indiana. He was a member of the " Long Session" of the Indiana Legislature, and voted for all the reforms which were characteristic of that session. He was city attorney in Chicago in 1860, under John Wentworth's administration; and since that time has devoted himself exclusively to his profession. Mr. King is tall, slender, with light complexion and blue eyes. He is a man of a good deal of brains, has a very lucrative general practice, ranks high as a jury lawyer, and is very much liked by those who know him.

THOMAS PARKER, JR.

THIS gentleman may be said to be a Western man, although born in Pennsylvania, as he was a child when removed to the West. He is now about twenty-six years old, and for twenty-four years has been a resident of Chicago. He received the best advantages the city afforded, then entered the University of Michigan, where he remained two years, but finished his education at the University of Chicago. Upon his graduation, he entered the Fifth National Bank as clerk, where he remained about a year, but a man of his mercurial temperament could not be long kept posting books and accounts. He threw up his situation, and entered the Chicago Law School, and in eight months from the time he began study, was admitted to the bar, and began the practice of the law. About four year since he became the junior partner in the firm of Ela & Parker.

The nervous temperament predominates; he is quick and lithe in movement, sharp in speech, apt in detecting an error, and rather merciless in exposing it. He is polished and refined in manner, is affable and social in a high degree, and possessing an ample fortune, enjoys life to the utmost. As a lawyer, he is shrewd and active, and, although a very young man as yet, has taken a good position as an acute and prompt business manager. His firm confines itself almost entirely to commercial law, and in its specialty is favorably known in other cities as well as Chicago.

JOHN W. ELA.

MR. ELA was born in Meredith, New Hampshire, and is about forty-five years of age. He received a liberal education in his native State, and entered the law school of Harvard, Mass., and graduated before he was twenty-one. On his return home, he became a partner of Judge Burroughs, of Plymouth, New Hampshire, with whom he remained until 1862, when he entered the army as Captain of the 15th N. H. Infantry. He was in active service about eighteen months, seeing in the time some of the hottest battles of the war, and was then appointed Provost Judge in the Gulf Department, which position he held until the close of the war.

At that time he came to Chicago and entered upon the practice of law.

As a lawyer, Mr. Ela occupies a prominent position, not only in Chicago, but throughout the State. He is equally good either in preparing a case, presenting it to a court, or before a jury. He is among the first of the profession as a man of integrity, industry and ability; and in Real Estate and Bankruptcy Law, of which he makes a specialty, he has perhaps few superiors. That he is successful, is shown by the fact that he is a real estate owner to some considerable extent in this city.

In private life Mr. Ela is highly esteemed for the many amiable qualities he possesses, no less than among the fraternity as a lawyer fo integrity and ability.

ISAAC G. WILSON.

Judge Wilson is a native of Western New York, and was born in 1816. He graduated from Brown University, Providence, R. I., in 1838. While in College, his father, Judge Wilson, removed to the West and settled in Northern Illinois. Upon his graduation, the son followed, and entered the office of Butterfield and Collins as a student. After remaining with them a year, he went to Cambridge, Mass., and entered the law school there. In 1841 he was admitted to the bar of Massachusetts, and immediately after returned to the West, to practice his profession. Finding Chicago possessed too large a proportion of professional men he pushed into the country and located at Elgin, in this State. In 1850, the 13th Circuit — known as the Kane Circuit — was created, and Mr. Wilson elected Judge, which office he continued to occupy until 1867, in all, seventeen years. Since leaving the bench Judge Wilson has been practicing in Chicago, and at present is senior of the firm of Wilson, Perry & Sturgis.

Such is the brief outline of a successful and honorable career. As lawyer, Judge and citizen, Mr. Wilson has possessed the unvarying esteem and confidence of all classes. He is a superior lawyer, well learned in the profession, and a notably successful chancery lawyer. He has no especial gifts as an advocate, but as counsellor is safe and reliable, and inclined to be pacific rather than belligerent. He seems to have a natural aptness for the duties of the judge in a mental organization that weighs and balances rather than originates and invents; and he can write an opinion better than he can make a speech.

He is well read, and converses fluently on any and all topics. He is inclined to be humorous, and relates the varied experiences which a long residence in the country, and many terms upon the bench have given, with an evident enjoyment.

Judge Wilson's social standing is fully equal to his professional status; and whether in public or private life, he commands the respect and wins the regard of the professional as well as the social world.

DANIEL GOODWIN, Jr.

THIS gentleman was born in New York City in 1832, and is the son of John W. and Lucretia Goodwin Woolsey, but at two years of age, losing his mother, he was adopted by his maternal uncle, Judge Daniel Goodwin, for whom he was named, and reared by him as his own son. He was prepared for college at Auburn, N. Y., entered Hamilton College in 1848, and graduated in 1852, taking the prizes in a class many of whom have achieved prominent positions at the bar, on the bench, and in the pulpit, as well as in politics and commerce. He studied law with Judge Goodwin in Detroit till 1853, then went to Auburn, N. Y., and in 1854 was admitted to the bar. He remained with his uncle, S. A. Goodwin, in Auburn, until 1855, when they both removed to Detroit, and formed a partnership with Judge Goodwin. In 1858 they came to Chicago, and entered at once into a large and lucrative practice. In 1864 Mr. Goodwin withdrew from the firm and practiced alone until 1867, when he formed a connection with A. L. Rockwell, which still exists, under the name of Goodwin & Rockwell.

Mr. Goodwin's practice has been general in character, but he has a decided preference for real estate law. Although he distinguished himself at college as an orator, he has a distaste for the wrangles of the court-room and the artifices of politics, which has had a tendency to keep him in the office rather than enter the noisy but more showy fields of labor.

Mr. Goodwin is somewhat distinguished as a writer, his pen never having been idle since his college days. He is noted also for his charitableness. There is not a movement of this nature which has applied to him in vain. His hand and brain and money are always ready, and in private charities his generosity is proverbial. He has been trustee of several institutions, and has occupied many positions of trust and importance both under the city and State governments, and has, under all circumstances, acquitted himself with honor and éclat.

His personal appearance is pleasing. He is refined in manner, polished in conversation, and at all times is a genial, courteous gentleman, whose intellectual attainments are admired by all who know him, while his kindness and generosity have endeared him to hosts of friends, and made him one of the most popular men at the Chicago bar.

MARLAND LESLIE PERKINS.

THIS young gentleman is the son of Dr. Perkins, of Fremont, Tazewell county, Illinois, and is now about thirty-five years old. He is tall, straight, and very dark, with straight black hair, which he wears thrown back, a keen, black eye, Roman nose, and high cheek bones Mr. Perkins claims a Mayflower-Indian princess pedigree, and looking at his strongly marked but handsome features, his erect, well-developed figure, swarthy, colorless complexion, and piercing eye, one may easily imagine they can recognize the mark of the Indian progenitor.

He was ready for college at the precocious age of twelve years, and entered the Freshman Class of Jubilee College, Illinois, at thirteen. He did not remain to graduate, deeming the studies prescribed by the Senior Course unnecessary and of no practical benefit. Leaving at the expiration of the Junior Course, he went to Bloomington and taught school a short time, then commenced the study of the law. He was admitted to the bar in 1859, and began practicing in Chicago, where he remained until September, 1861, when he enlisted in the Ninth Illinois Cavalry, winning a brilliant reputation as a faithful and daring officer. The last six months of his term of service was spent at Memphis, as Judge Advocate of the District of West Tennessee. In 1864 he was mustered out of the service, his term having expired, and remained in Memphis, determined to reside there and practice his profession. Soon after, he was tendered by General Washburn, Commander of the District of Tennessee, the office of Judge of the Civil Commission, which in the disorganized state of affairs during the war, took the place of the Common Law Court, which he accepted and filled acceptably until the re-establishment of the regular courts. In 1867 he was appointed United States District Attorney by President Johnson, but his appointment was not confirmed by the Senate. In 1871 Mr. Perkins returned to Chicago and resumed practice in this city. He is now of the firm of Merriam, Alexander and Perkins.

As a lawyer Mr. Perkins is well spoken of by his seniors and associates, and is looked upon as a man who is making his mark among the thousand aspirants for pre-eminence in the profession. His tastes incline toward admiralty and real estate practice, in which he is very successful. He is a fluent speaker, witty in conversation, quick at *repartee*, elegant in dress, and rather elaborately courteous in manner.

DANIEL GOODWIN.

JUDGE GOODWIN, who for more than forty years occupied a distinguished position as lawyer and Judge, and before whom many of the Chicago bar have practiced in the courts of Michigan, is one whose learning, ability and purity have been admtred by all who were brought in contact with him. He was the eldest child of Dr. Daniel Goodwin, of Geneva, N. Y.; graduated at the head of his class in 1820; studied law with J. C. Spencer, of New York. He removed to Detroit in 1828, and was United States Attorney under Presidents Jackson and Van Buren. In 1843 he was made Judge of the Supreme court of Michigan. In 1850 was President of the Constitutional Convention, and member of the convention of 1865. In 1855 he was re-elected Judge of the District Court for the upper peninsula of Michigan, and again in 1856, in 1862, and in 1868.

He is a man of remarkable astuteness as a lawyer and unblemished probity as a Judge and politician. In private as in public life, his name has been untarnished by so much as a breath, and his life a monument of good deeds.

EDWARD J. HILL.

Mr. Hill, who is perhaps more remarkable as a writer than a practitioner, is a native of New York, and is now about forty years old. He graduated from the University of Vermont in the class of 1843. He then read law, but turned his attention to banking, then to general merchandise, forwarding and shipping, by which means he acquired a thorough understanding of commercial matters.

His practice as a lawyer did not commence until about 1859 or 1860, when he opened an office at Milwaukee. He succeeded admirably, and soon won an enviable reputation as a skillful and persistent lawyer. In 1869 he came to Chicago, and bids fair to attain eminence in the two-fold character of writer and practitioner. As a counselor he is much esteemed by his clients, and he avoids rather than seeks litigation.

More recently, Mr. Hill has left the beaten track, the practice in the courts, and turned his attention to theoretical law. He has already given to the public three volumes which competent judges pronounce the most thorough and practical works ever produced this side of the Atlantic. They constitute a complete set of practice works, adapted to the Law of Procedure in this State. No other State has adhered more closely to English practice than Illinois. The practice here is, therefore, of great practical value, for it rests on English precedent, and involves the entire scope and history of English jurisprudence.

In style Mr. Hill is terse and vigorous, apt in his illustrations, accurate and concise in statement, with no unnecessary repetition — an incredible statement to the uninitiated reader of legal lore.

In this brief notice of Mr. Hill's books is sketched the mental characteristics of the man. He is studious and industrious, and possesses a patience and coolness temperamentally that finds pleasure in exhuming, analyzing, comparing and deducing, — a most laborious mental process unless adapted to it by nature.

HAMILTON N. ELDRIDGE.

GENERAL ELDRIDGE was born in South Williamstown, Berkshire county, Massachusetts, and is now thirty-eight years of age. His father was a farmer, and during the Mexican war held the rank of Colonel. His son, fitted for college at East Hampton, in Massachusetts, entered Williams in 1852, and graduated four years later, taking the first prize of his class for elocution. He studied law under Judge Ira Harris, and his brother, Hamilton Harris, in Albany, New York, and graduated at the law school in the same place in 1857. He came to Chicago the same year, and went into the office of Baker & Hyatt, after which he began practice by himself. In 1858 he formed a partnership with F. W. Tourtellotte, and with whom he has been associated ever since, under the name of Eldridge & Tourtellotte.

In 1862 he entered the volunteer service as Lieutenant-Colonel of the 127th Illinois infantry; and three weeks later he took command of the regiment, and was promoted to Colonel in the same year. At the battle of Arkansas Post, he and his regiment were first inside the Confederate works; and at the battles before Vicksburg, in May, 1863, he took the colors, after all the color-guard had been shot down, and led his regiment, for which act of gallantry he was made a Brevet Brigadier-General. Since his retirement from the army, General Eldridge has assiduously devoted himself to the practice of the legal profession.

He is above medium height, with light hair and eyes, regular features and full beard. In his manners he is very finished, and possesses affability and sociability in a very high degree. He has a decided literary taste, and is not only especially fond of poetry, but a poet of no mean order, finding in pursuits of this nature rest and recreation. He has also a remarkable memory, and can repeat *verbatum et literatum* from all the classic poets, to a degree limited only by his leisure and inclination.

As a lawyer, he occupies a very conspicuous position. His practice, and that of his firm, is a general one, embracing every variety of cases; in a single morning may be seen in their office the millionaire and the day laborer, the doctor of divinity and the professional swindler, each waiting for advice or to pay a retainer. He has been engaged in a good many very important cases, among which the most notorious one was the suit of Amanda J. Craig against Elisha C. Sprague, for breach of promise, and in which the firm of which he is a member obtained the largest verdict ever known in suits for damages — $100,000. His success in this suit was won by the same indefatigable industry, the same care in the preparation of the case, and the same devotion which he shows to the interests of his clients in all his practice. He is not only a successful practitioner, but a thoroughly intelligent lawyer, and a liberal, courteous gentleman.

F. W. TOURTELLOTTE.

This gentleman is of the old French Hugonot stock; his ancestors having been driven to America in the seventeenth century by reason of religious persecution and intolerance. He was born in Windham county, Connecticut, and received a thorough classical and scientific education in the best schools of his native State and of Massachusetts. He afterwards graduated with high honors at the Albany Law University. Immediately thereafter, in 1857, he removed to Joliet and commenced the practice of law; from whence, on the following year, he removed to Chicago and formed a law partnership with General H. N. Eldridge, where he has remained in the active practice of his profession, with scarcely an exception, until the present time, having succeeded, in the meanwhile, in establishing and maintaining an exceedingly remunerative and extensive legal business, an achievement in this city requiring other elements of success than mere luck.

Mr. Tourtellotte was elected Major of the 127th regiment of Illinois volunteers, during the late war of the Rebellion, but was compelled, much against his wishes, to decline the commission. He has never been a partisan politician, and has always steadily refused all official patronage.

Mr. Tourtellotte is wholly absorbed in the business of his profession, into which he directs all his energies and skill. He is in the general practice, so called, making a specialty, as yet, of no particular branch of the law, if we may except commercial law, and perhaps cases arising under insurance and bankrupt laws. One of his chief characteristics as a practicing attorney is the versatility of his legal talents. Whether in the Circuit Courts of the United States, in the argument of an abstruse question of constitutional law, in the courts of Admiralty, in the various courts of the State, or before a jury, he seems equally ready and efficient.

He never allows the claims of a client to suffer at his hands, if hard work, and all his legal skill can prevent it, for he prepares his cases with great care, and thoroughly masters the legal principles involved therein. As an advocate, and in the trial of a cause, whether civil or criminal, his reputation is excellent; and his efficiency therein is nowhere more particularly exemplified than in his ability to frustrate the positions of his antagonist, and to turn them to his own advantage.

He is a close student, and has the reputation among his legal brethren of possessing an extensive acquaintance with nearly all branches of the law; he is familiar with the details of practice, and has a thorough knowledge of business and men.

Mr. Tourtellotte is painstaking and laborious in whatever direction his professional services may be employed; and he has proved himself an indispensable auxiliary in the important and extended interests committed to the firm of which he is a member. As a lawyer he has a rising reputation, which the large number of important causes constantly being committed to the care and management of the firm to which he belongs abundantly proves. Nor is his reputation a local one. The docket of his firm contains the names of clients from all parts of the great Northwest, and in nearly every State court therein.

This gentleman is thirty-five years of age, over six feet in height, with an erect figure, and an agreeable and expressive countenance. He is dignified in his bearing, affable in his manners, fluent in his speech, active and graceful in his movements, and ambitious of success. A little energetic, it may be, sometimes, in his gestures and expressions, when, in the heat of debate, or otherwise, an opponent is to be rebuked, ignorance to be exposed, or craft to be thwarted, but never aggressive or unnecessarily severe. Sociability and a faultless generosity are distinguishing traits in his character.

In the management of the celebrated case of Craig *vs.* Sprague he took an active and prominent part, and it was owing to his industry and superb management, as also the firm to which he belongs, that a result was achieved than which there has been none more remarkable or successful in the record of litigation.

E. W. EVANS.

Mr. Evans was born in Fryburg, Oxford county, Maine; received a preparatory course at the Fryburg Academy, and graduated at Dartmouth College in the class of 1838.

Immediately after his graduation he entered the law office of Judge Chase, in Hopkinton, N. H., where he remained until he was admitted to the bar.

In 1840, he came West, where he has since remained, devoting himself to the practice of law with a singleness of purpose and industry that have placed him at the head of the profession, and secured him a very substantial pecuniary position. There is probably not another man among the fraternity who is so thoroughly the lawyer as Mr. Evans. Although possessing every qualification requisite to the successful politician, he has persistently refused every inducement to enter the political field, and prides himself upon the fact that he has never allowed himself to be a candidate for any political office. In October, 1871, he received a letter, couched in the most complimentary language and signed by many of the prominent lawyers of the city, asking him to become a candidate for the office of Judge of the Circuit Court of Cook County.

Mr. Evans is a very decided character, as well as a lawyer of very excellent ability. In manners, dress and appearance, he belongs to the old school of gentlemen, so few of whom now remain.

He is genial and courteous in his personal and professional relations. In these he stands so well with the brethren of the bar that he is frequently retained, at their instance, to lead them in their own cases. He is always earnest, forcible and effective as a speaker, sometimes rises into eloquence, and knows how to wield the weapon of invective to a purpose. He summons and commands his resources readily for an emergency, and especially is skilled in cross-examination and in eliciting the full truth from any witness, however determined he may be to conceal the same; and, generally, with his ability and success in trying cases, is a first-class jury lawyer. Some of his later cases evince this fact conspicuously. Particularly the noted cases of Wilkinson vs. The Chicago Tribune, a libel suit in which his printed speech remains to attest his oratory, and the Zeigenmeyer murder case, in which he distinguished himself. He has been very successful in suits for damages growing out of personal injuries, and brought against corporations, railroad and municipal; and there are few at the bar who can aspire to rival him in this class of cases.

His arguments in the Supreme Court are as effective, generally, as his speeches to the jury. In these he displays the finest specimens of his logic and the amplest stores of his learning, and he may well pride himself on the success which usually attends him in the court of last resort. He is a great reader, and a gentleman of culture outside of his profession, and devotes all his leisure moments to general literature.

THOS. J. TURNER.

THOMAS JOHNSTON TURNER was born in Trumbull county, Ohio, on the 5th day of April, A.D. 1815. The country at that time was almost an unbroken forest, yet with the enterprise which characterized the "Western Reserve," the log school-house followed the pioneer into the deepest recesses of the wilderness, and at the age of ten years Mr. Turner had acquired something of a common-school education. At that time he removed, with his parents, to Butler county, Penn., where, owing to the necessities of the family, he was put to work at farming. At the age of eighteen he left home, and traveled on foot to Chicago, ariving there about the 1st of May, A.D. 1833, but finding Chicago little else than a swamp, he returned to La Porte county, Indiana, where he remained until he was twenty-one years old, when, mainly by his efforts, his father's family were removed to the West and comfortably settled. This done, he struck out for himself. He spent one year in Dubuque and Western Wisconsin, engaged in mining and building bellows for the first blast furnaces built in the lead mines. In the spring of 1836, having accumulated a little money, he settled in Stephenson county, Illinois, and engaged in the building of mills, but in the fall of 1837, the floods having swept away his mills and left him largely in debt, he turned his attention to the study of law. At this time he had picked up a sort of general education from close study of such books as came within his reach. In the spring of 1840 he was admitted to the bar, and settled in Freeport, where he soon secured an excellent practice, and held the offices of Justice of the Peace and Probate Justice. About this time Mr. Turner was appointed State's Attorney by Governor Ford, and he at once entered upon the discharge of its duties, and became very successful in bringing to justice offenders. During his term of office the gang of thieves and robbers which infested the Rock River country were broken up, and the murderers of Colonel Davenport tried and executed. In 1846 Mr. Turner was elected to Congress upon the Democratic ticket, where he served one term, and then retired to the practice of law. In 1854 he was elected to the State Legislature, and made Speaker of the House of Representatives. He was a member of the Peace Conference in 1861; returning from Washington, he was made Colonel of the Fifteenth Regiment Illinois Volunteers, and had the first three years' regiment mustered into the service. He soon after took command of a camp of instruction at Alton; afterwards commanded a brigade, and then the First Division of the Army of the West. He remained in the service until the fall of 1862, when he was forced to resign on account of ill health. After his health was restored he resumed the practice of law. He was elected a member of the Convention to revise the Constitution of Illinois in 1870, and rendered efficient service in the adoption of most of the reforms in that instrument. In 1871 he was elected to the lower house of the General Assembly, and was the Democratic candidate for United States Senator against General Logan, the Republican candidate. In July, 1871, Mr. Turner opened an office in Chicago, where he now resides. Until coming to Chicago his practice extended over a number of counties, and included all classes of cases. His tastes and habits incline him to chancery, in which department he has had an extensive practice. As a lawyer, Col. Turner is careful, painstaking and reliable.

He has a refined, scholarly face, and in manner he is dignified and suave. He is a devoted reader still, and a good deal of a bibliophilist, having possessed, at the time of the fire, one of the best selected libraries in the West.

JOHN V. LE MOYNE.

This gentleman is a native of Pennsylvania, and is now about forty-five years of age. His father was a prominent politician and an old resident of Washington county, and Mr. Le Moyne received the two-fold advantage of good scholastic training and the early association of cultured, thinking men. He graduated from Washington College in 1847; studied law and was admitted to the bar in Pittsburgh, Pennsylvania, and came directly to Chicago, where he has been long and favorably known as a lawyer of excellent standing and ability. He is thoroughly well read, and is equally effective before a jury or presenting an argument before a court, and is a very assiduous and successful practitioner.

Mr. Le Moyne is rather over the medium size, and rather heavily built. He has black hair and eyes, and a countenance indicative of force of character, and in manner he is agreeable and cultivated.

JOHN J. McKINNON.

This gentleman was born in Charleston, South Carolina, and received his preparatory education there. He is a graduate of the Jesuit College of Georgetown, District of Columbia, also of St. Rheims, France. Upon his return from Europe, he studied law with Nicholas Hill, of Albany, New York, and then with Christian Rozilius, of New Orleans, and finally with Swett & Orme, in Bloomington, Illinois. He came to Chicago from New York in 1848, and has since resided in the West.

Mr. McKinnon is a lawyer of very superior abilities, who is well versed in his profession, and who has been intrusted with several very important cases in the Supreme Court of the United States. He is accorded by the fraternity a fine legal mind, and is probably one of the most cultured gentlemen at the bar. He converses fluently in several languages, and is thoroughly familiar with the classics. His face is intelligent and pleasing, and his manner has the courtly finish for which educated Southerners have been so long and justly celebrated.

WILLIAM H. RICHARDSON.

Mr. Richardson was born in Strykersville, New York, in 1840. He was educated at Andover, Massachusetts, and graduated from college in 1861. Soon after he came to Chicago and entered the office of Knox, Eustace & Reed, as a law student, and in 1863 was admitted to the bar. In 1865 he entered into a partnership with Mr. Reed, which continued until the election of Mr. Reed as District Attorney. Upon the dissolution of the firm, Mr. Richardson succeeded to the business, and by close attention and his superior attainments has not only kept but added to the large practice.

Mr. Richardson has a predilection for criminal practice, and in his chosen field is particularly successful. In conducting a case he prefers to quietly accomplish by strategic flank movment, outside, what others attempt by direct assault with a flourish of trumpets in open court. Mr. Richardson has also a very happy faculty of giving his clients such satisfaction that, although still a comparatively young man, there are few members of the bar who have a more lucrative practice.

SAMUEL M. MOORE.

This gentleman was born in Bourbon county, Kentucky. He studied law at Cynthiana, in that State, under the Hon. James Curry, one of the oldest and most accurate lawyers in the State. Judge Moore commenced his professional career in 1843. In 1845 he removed to Covington, Ky., and soon became one of the ablest and most eminent members of the bar of that city.

In 1856 he was elected Judge of the ninth judicial circuit of Kentucky. In becoming a candidate for this office, he refused to accept the nomination of any political party, or to electioneer for it, and while on the bench, studiously avoided taking any part in party politics, believing that the purity and impartiality of the judiciary demanded that, as far as practicable, it should be kept aloof from the contamination of partizan political influences. On the bench Judge Moore was distinguished for the soundness of his decisions and remarkable industry and rapidity in the dispatch of business. It was his custom, when the state of the docket required it, to devote the day to the trial of law causes, and a large portion of the night to the hearing and decision of chancery cases, and such was his rapidity that he would often hear and dispose of a half dozen cases in one night, and the next morning bring his decrees in all of them into court, written out with his own hand, which he preferred to do to avoid the possibility of error, and these decrees were seldom appealed from or reversed. In this way the business of all his courts was constantly kept up, to the great satisfaction of the bar and the benefit of the community.

At the close of the late war, his judicial term having expired, he removed to Chicago and entered into his present law partnership with the Hon. B. Caulfield, then in full practice. At the bar he has also been distinguished by the same untiring industry, and by a clear comprehension of legal principles, and an accurate application of them to the facts of a case. His firm enjoys a large practice.

Judge Moore is a fine specimen of Kentucky growth, with a large and massive head, and a countenance beaming with intelligence and amiability. He has long been a prominent and influential member of the Presbyterian Church, filling the office of a ruling elder, and regarded by his Church as a man of sterling piety and integrity of character. In politics he has been a life-long Democrat, and in Kentucky was one of the most influential leaders of his party, though since his location in Chicago he has declined to take any active part in political matters, devoting himself exclusively to the business of his profession. He is now about fifty years of age.

JOHN H. PECK.

This gentleman was born in Lyme, Connecticut, in 1832. He received a good general education in the schools of his native town, and studied law at the Yale Law School, New Haven. He was admitted to the bar at Norwich, Connecticut, in November, 1852. In 1853 he came to Chicago and entered upon the practice of his profession. In 1861 he entered the army as Lieutenant, and served four years. He was mustered out of the service in August, 1865, as Colonel, with an unblemished record, and immediately resumed his professional labors in this city.

Mr. Peck has a very extensive practice as the result of many years' close application to business. He is an acute lawyer, active and influential in politics, and genial in conversation and manner.

JULIUS P. ATWOOD

was born in Monkton, Vermont, in 1825; was educated at the Norwich University; read law with Judge Rich, of the Supreme Court of that State, and commenced its practice with Hon. Wm. C. Wilson, afterwards Judge of the same court; and was for two or three years, and until he removed to Madison, Wisconsin, in 1861, Professor in the Franklin Law School at Bakersfield, Vermont. In 1854 he was appointed Judge of the Dane County Court, and held that position for two and a half years, when ill health compelled him to resign. He was Chairman of the Democratic State Central Committee, and in 1859 was named by the Democratic members of the Legislature as candidate for Judge of the Supreme Court, but he declined to run, and in 1860 was Democratic candidate for State Attorney; was Democratic candidate for Mayor at the first municipal election at Madison. He organized the Governor's Guard in 1857, and soon after went to the Potomac as Lieutenant-Colonel of the Sixth Regiment, infantry, but was early disabled and compelled to leave. For two years he was partially paralyzed, and after his recovery settled in Chicago, and returned to the practice of the law. Judge Atwood is a well educated lawyer, and a gentleman of more than ordinary literary attainments. In argument he is direct, close and severe, but it is the severity of logic. He is eminently courteous at the bar, and incapable of doing any one injury. In popular addresses he is terse and methodical, often impassioned and sometimes eloquent. The lawyers from Wisconsin, resident here, with unanimity requested him to run for Circuit Judge last fall, but he declined the honor. He is of medium height, affable and dignified, and his professional and personal character is one that commands universal respect.

A. W. WINDETT.

This lawyer is one of the best read, accurate and acute members of the Chicago bar; and in the department of Chancery practice he has few equals and no superiors. At heart, Mr. Windett is a very thorough gentleman; in the practice of his profession it sometimes happens that his zeal leads him into a mannerism which, to say the least, is almost aggressive. He is very forcible and determined. His practice is a large one, and includes many cases of very high importance. While there may be other lawyers who are more popular in the profession, there are none whose abilities command a wider respect. He is about forty-three years of age, and has been here since 1857.

EDWIN C. LARNED,

of the firm of Goodwin, Larned & Towle, is a well-known lawyer of great ability. He was United States District Attorney under Mr. Lincoln. At present he remains much away from Chicago, and gives but little attention to general practice. He is a man of great wealth and cultivation, and once occupied a very distinguished position as a member of the legal profession.

A. H. LAWRENCE

is a partner of E. G. Asay, is a native of Massachusetts, is a tall, good-looking gentleman, twenty-eight years of age, and a young man of very decided promise. He devotes himself closely to his profession, and will, in due season, be heard from as a member of the bar in this city.

D. K. TENNEY.

This gentleman was born in Plattsburgh, N. Y., on the last day of the year 1834, and is the tenth and youngest child of his parents. In his infancy he was carried "in arms" to northern Ohio, then a wilderness. At the age of eight he entered the "poor boy's college," — a printing office — and continued there with little interruption until, fifteen years of age, when he removed to Madison, Wisconsin, and entered the University at that place. Here, with the pittance earned in vacations, as a printer, he struggled through three years of study, taking high rank as a scholar. Becoming tired of his penniless condition, he deserted his *alma mater* and commenced the study of law. In 1855, at the age of twenty, he was admitted to the bar at Madison, and opened an office there. From that time until his removal to Chicago, in 1870, he continued to enjoy an active, successful, and lucrative practice, and acquired, through an honorable career, and without adventitious aid, a handsome competence, which he still enjoys.

Mr. Tenney is a self-made man, and of a peculiarly Western

type. He wears his rough side out, having an unpolished manner, and paying little regard to conventionalities, or to a choice of fine language to express himself. He may be said to be a "lion" or a "lamb," as the occasion requires, for beneath the rough exterior he possesses and is governed by as fine feelings, and is as emotional and gentle as a woman. He is considerably above the average stature, has a fine physical construction, a large and intensely active brain, and a fine nervous temperament. Is open hearted, generous and kind, eminently social, when at leisure, and is possessed of a readiness of wit and fund of anecdote, and a unique manner of giving utterance to them which render him quite notable among his intimate friends. He is not lacking in public spirit, but despises politics and politicians, yet usually backs his favorite candidate with a reasonable figure.

As a lawyer, Mr. Tenney is thoroughly practical, and is noted for his keen perception of what the law ought to be. He entertains a poor opinion of the slow processes of courts, and leaves the trial of causes mainly to his partners more able in that direction. He excels in the office as a manager of the business, and as a counselor and negotiator, and prefers an amicable settlement upon fair terms to the procrastination and doubtful result of a trial. Where a grace cannot be negotiated, he is most vigilant and untiring in marshalling the facts and the witnesses to sustain his cause, leaving the law more especially to his colleagues. As a negotiator and counselor in mercantile difficulties, and as a collector of doubtful and desperate debts, his long experience and success have won him truly great fame. He has no superiors and probably few equals in this branch of the profession, as many of our merchants and business men testify. In fine, he is a sound business lawyer, of scrupulous honor and integrity, a warm friend, and an outspoken enemy.

Mr. Tenney is of the firm of Tenney, McClellan & Tenney, one of the leading ones of the city in commercial law.

JOSEPH F. BONFIELD,

who is indigenous to Chicago, having been born here, and having acquired the profession in this city, is a young man of liberal, general education, an excellent lawyer, apt before a jury, and has a very extended practice, which is largely made up of real estate litigation.

With him is associated Warren J. Durham, who was formerly connected with Hon. Henry Fuller, of Racine. Mr. Durham is a well-read, accurate lawyer; and is a fine linguist, and a classical scholar of a very peculiar kind.

DANIEL J. SCHUYLER.

This gentleman was born near Amsterdam, N. Y. He is the son of a wealthy farmer, and as his name indicates, a member of one of the oldest of the Knickerbocker families, so well known in the history of New York. He received a liberal education, being a graduate of Union College; studied law with the Hon. Francis Kernan, of Utica, N. Y.; was admitted to the bar in 1864, and immediately after came to Chicago to enter upon the practice of his profession.

His personal appearance is prepossessing. He is about thirty years of age, is of average height, and compactly built. His features are regular and clear cut, indicating reticence, niceness of perception and perseverance rather than aggressive power, while his manner shows the quiet, well-bred gentleman.

As a lawyer, Mr. Schuyler is well liked by other members of the bar, and is universally spoken of as a rising man. There is nothing of the meteoric in his course, but a steady progress that promises much for his future; and while his present attainments, both as a scholar and a lawyer, are of no mean order, there are heights beyond, which his fine mental endowments and indefatigable industry will enable him to reach.

JOHN L. THOMPSON.

When the war broke out, General Thompson, then a student in the office of McCagg & Fuller, enlisted with the thirty-day volunteers, and went to Cairo. At the expiration of his term of service he went to New Hampshire and enlisted as a private soldier. He soon rose to the rank of Colonel, and to the command of a regiment of cavalry. He served during the war, and received the rank of Brigadier-General. After the war he came to Chicago, and went into the practice of law. As a lawyer, although a young man, he takes a very creditable position. He is well posted in law, is very industrious and attentive, very cautious; and, if he has a noticeable fault, it is that he is inclined to give more attention to what may be presented by an opponent than to his own resources for offense or defense. He has a large amount of force and character, and has a business that includes some of the best men in Chicago.

JAMES H. ROBERTS.

This gentleman has been in practice here some fifteen years. He is a very close student, a well-read lawyer, and a good general practitioner. As an office lawyer he is very superior, and is a gentleman of thorough morality and integrity.

JOSEPH A. SLEEPER.

This gentleman is about forty-five years of age. He is tall, angular, and somewhat of the Lincoln style of architecture — bony, disjointed and awkward. He bears the appearance of a studious, painstaking lawyer. He came to Chicago from Wisconsin about eight years ago, and brought with him a very excellent reputation in his profession. He is very thoroughly versed in common law, and has the credit of being a chancery lawyer of high order. He is rather better as an office lawyer than before a jury, although he is very forcible in the latter character. He is well grounded in law, and his opinions are valuable and carefully prepared. He has been employed in many suits of importance, and has met with good success. He stands well, and his prospects are good for further progress.

BERNARD G. CAULFIELD.

This gentleman was born in Alexandria, Virginia, and first came into notice as a *protegé* of Father Matthews, a well known and wealthy Catholic clergyman of Washington. Mr. Caulfield was educated at the college of Georgetown. After graduating he went to Kentucky and studied law at the Transylvania University. He removed from Kentucky to Chicago in 1854.

Mr. Caulfield is a lawyer of considerable merit. His most salient trait is his great courtesy. He is a finished gentleman as well as lawyer. In his speeches he is deliberate, careful of the selection of his phrases, and clear and forcible in the presentation of his ideas.

He is erect, full-bearded, with dark eyes, and an intelligent head. His personal appearance coincides very exactly with his cultivated manners; and he seems equally at home whether in the *rôle* of a lawyer pleading a case before a jury, or as a private citizen interchanging hospitalities at the social board. He is in great demand among our Irish citizens, and is always put forward by them when there is anything to be done that requires to be done well, elegantly, and intelligently.

U. P. SMITH.

This gentleman is about thirty-six years of age. He is tall, slender, with dark eyes, an intelligent, prepossessing face, and a full, dark beard. He is a member of the firm of Walker, Dexter & Smith, and is a lawyer of unquestionable ability, both with reference to his knowledge of law, and as an advocate. He has very remarkable powers as a reader of character, and in the faculty of expressing his conclusions. He already stands high at the bar, and there is every probability that he will, and soon, place himself in the very front rank of the profession in the West.

PHILIP HOYNE.

Mr. Hoyne was born in New York, in about 1826. He was admitted to the bar in Chicago in 1855, but only practiced some three years. He was elected Clerk of the Recorder's Court, and since closing his law practice, he has been entirely engaged in his duties as United States Commissioner, a position which he still holds. Mr. Hoyne is a portly, good-looking gentleman, and enjoys a very general popularity.

OLIVER H. HORTON

was born in the State of New York in 1835, where he remained until 1855, when he left school and at once came to this city. From that time till 1860 he was engaged, as many of Chicago's young men have been who came here poor, alone and among strangers, in earning an honest livelihood by his own exertions. But this does not seem to have been lost time with him. During this time, the transitory period from boyhood to manhood, this susceptible period in every man's life in which so many in our great cities yield to surrounding temptations, he formed habits which added very much to his success as a lawyer.

In the spring of 1860 he entered the law office of Messrs. Hoyne, Miller & Lewis, as a student. With this firm he remained, as student and then clerk, until January 1864, when that firm was dissolved. Immediately upon such dissolution, he entered into a partnership with Hon. Thomas Hoyne, which is continued to the present time.

Although not a collegiate, Mr. Horton had a liberal education, and was a very ardent student, being absent from the office but a day or two while a student. Two years of this time he was a member of the Law School of the University of Chicago, under the instruction of Judge Booth, now of the Circuit Court, from which institution he graduated in 1863, having, however, been previously, during the same year, admitted to the bar.

Upon entering into practice, it was very soon seen that by his four years of close application as a student, he was prepared to cope successfully with those already at the bar. His case is another illustration of the fact to which most, if not all the older members of the profession will attest, that good lawyers are not made or properly fitted for practice in a year.

Mr. Horton has, during his practice of nearly eight years, been engaged in many important suits, and no young man of the same years' experience enjoys a more enviable reputation. By those who know him best he is most highly esteemed. He never condescends to any of the low tricks practiced by some who have fastened themselves upon the profession. To his legal attainments may be added the fact of his sterling integrity. Being of a stern and positive turn he may sometimes offend, but never wounds.

ROBERT T. LINCOLN.

This young gentleman is a son of the late President Lincoln, and is a very worthy, estimable member of the Chicago bar. He is but a little more than twenty-five years of age, and already has taken a position as being an excellent manager, possessed of good ability, quiet, shrewd, unostentatious, and with a thorough devotion to the profession of law. He is the more entitled to credit from the fact that he steadily resisted all attempts to induce him to accept some official position while his father was President, or to participate in politics since; and that he has applied himself to his legal studies precisely as if he were the son of the least influential of parents, and has pursued them under many painful and most discouraging circumstances. He has proved that he has a thousand sterling qualities, and there can be no doubt that with age he will attain a distinguished eminence as a member of the legal profession.

ROBERT RAE

is a slender, handsome gentleman of some forty or forty-five years of age. He is very finished in his dress and personal appearance, and confines himself in law almost or quite wholly to admiralty affairs, in which he confessedly stands at the head of the profession.

J. A. CRAM *

is believed by some of his professional brethren to be one of the most able and promising young lawyers at the Chicago bar. He is about thirty-seven years of age, is very modest, quiet and unostentatious in his bearing, and at heart a thoroughly honorable and estimable gentleman.

D. J. LYON.

Mr. Lyon was born in New Orleans, graduated in the law department of the Chicago University, and is in the general practice of law. He possesses to some extent the peculiar Southern characteristics. He is graceful in manner, and is a fluent and impressive speaker. As a lawyer he is industrious, energetic, reliable, and possesses ability which will secure him a high position at the bar. Mr. Lyon is genial and gentlemanly, and has many friends among the profession and elsewhere.

S. D. PHELPS.

This is a young and rising lawyer, who is a graduate from the law office of Goodrich, Farwell & Smith. He was admitted in 1866,

* Since deceased.

and has been in practice since that time, except during the last winter, when he was in the Legislature. He has been very largely engaged in revenue cases, but now is in general practice. He is a very fluent, easy and graceful speaker, and promises to take a very excellent position as an advocate.

LESTER L. BOND

was born in Ravenna, Ohio, in 1830, passed his early life on a farm, and in the practical study of the mechanical arts. With only a good common school education, and a few terms at the village academy, he applied himself to the study of law and was admitted to the bar in 1853, practiced in Ravenna for one year, and removed to Chicago in 1854, and engaged at first in the general practice of law. His practical knowledge of mechanical arts and inventions, and his natural fondness for the study of mechanics, chemistry, and kindred sciences, soon induced him to select the law pertaining to patents as a specialty, and to the study and practice of this he applied himself with unremitting industry. In 1866 he formed a copartnership with Hon. Edmund A. West, formerly of Wisconsin, and the firm of West & Bond are now engaged in nearly every litigated patent case in Chicago and vicinity, and has achieved an enviable reputation in Washington, New York, and other eastern cities.

Mr. Bond was a member of the Common Council from 1863 to 1866; served in the Legislature in sessions of 1867 and 1869; was a member of the Board of Education for several years, and in all these positions won general respect and confidence. In his manners Mr. Bond is genial and courteous, but modest and undemonstrative. Thoroughly conscientious in private life, he carries integrity and honor into his professional duties, and will employ no chicanery to secure a dishonorable victory. His suits are fairly contested and his victories fairly won. His temperament is inclined to the phlegmatic, and as a thinker he is clear and logical rather than rapid. He possesses a memory tenacious both of principles and facts, and has a rare faculty of correct judgment. With varied self-culture and reserve power in many directions he was capable of attaining eminence in other pursuits, but has wisely chosen that for which he is peculiarly fitted, and as a patent lawyer he is now the peer of any member of the bar in the West, and has few superiors in the country.

JOHN MASON

is a lawyer who has attained a good deal of eminence in the department of criminal practice, in which direction his success has been fully equal to that of many members of the Chicago bar. He is the successor of the noted Pat. Ballingall, of a former generation. He is of Irish birth, is about forty-five years of age, and has a very slender body compared to the extent and force of his intellect.

FREDERICK SACKETT.

This gentleman is a native of Westfield, Massachusetts, at which place he received his earlier education. At the age of twenty-three he represented his native town in the legislature of the State. Having entered upon the study of the law, and finding himself embarrassed for means to prosecute his studies, he concluded to try his fortunes in California, and in 1849 he joined the thousands who in that year made the overland trip to the Pacific coast. This trip was a reasonably successful one for him, as it freed him from his embarrassments as a student, and enabled him to prosecute his studies under highly favorable circumstances. Upon his return he entered the law office of Thompson & Weeks, of Poughkeepsie, New York, where he remained for about three years. Upon his admission to the bar in 1853 he located in Sterling, Illinois, where he soon achieved an enviable reputation, and for many years, and up to the period of his removal to Chicago in the spring of 1869, was regarded as at the head of the profession in his circuit. Besides being a counselor of acknowledged ability, he is a trial lawyer of unusual excellence. In argument he is clear, forcible, and effective; and while he enforces his points with earnestness, he is uniformly respectful to court and jury, and courteous toward opposing counsel and parties. His eminent fairness and candor, and acknowledged probity of character, inspire confidence, and his opinions command universal respect.

GEORGE GARDINER.

This gentleman has very many fine qualifications. He has very excellent judgment, is a faithful and reliable adviser, and an able counsellor, and is a gentleman who stands exceedingly well with the profession.

ROBERT H. FORRESTER.

Mr. Forrester was born at Pittsburgh, Pennsylvania, of Scottish parents, his father having been an eminent scholar and professor of mathematics, and a graduate of the University of Edinburgh. He studied law at Pittsburgh under the Hon. James Dunlop. After his admission to the bar he practiced about two years in the courts of Pittsburg, acquiring, especially in criminal practice, the reputation of a rising young lawyer of fair promise. In 1846, he emigrated to the State of Kentucky, and soon afterwards was placed at the head of a flourishing law school connected with a college at Georgetown, Ky., which he conducted for several years, Speaker Blaine, of the present House of Representatives, then a professor in the same college, having been one of his pupils. Afterwards he practiced his profession in the courts of the famous "Blue Grass" region of Kentucky, of which Lexington is the central city, enjoying the reputation of a sound and laborious lawyer, and holding the position in the old Whig party of an earnest and eloquent advocate of Whig principles, but, eschewing all aspirations to office, chose to devote himself exclusively to his profession.

A short time before the late war he removed into the cotton country of the South, and became a cotton planter in Alabama, though still actively pursuing the practice of law. In 1864, at the solicitation of the friends of Peace and the restoration of the Union, then a large party in the State of Georgia, including such men as Joshua Hill, Alexander H. Stephens, and Joseph Brown, Mr. Forrester assumed the position of editor-in-chief of the "Augusta Chronicle and Sentinel," published at Augusta, Georgia, and the newspaper organ of the Peace party in that State. As the editor of this paper, he wrote many able and pungent editorial articles in favor of peace and an immediate return to the Union, and against the administration and suicidal policy of Jefferson Davis, which were extensively read and commented on throughout the South, and exerted a powerful influence on the public mind. In his editorial contests he frequently grappled with such master spirits of the Southern press as Pollard, of the "Richmond Examiner," and other champions of Jefferson Davis, and in the course of this newspaper warfare, which for a year waged fiercely, he wrote a lengthy and elaborate reply to an address of the famous Howell Cobb to the people of Georgia, in defence of the suspension of the writ of *habeas corpus* by the Richmond

Government. The only reply which Mr. Cobb, or his friends, ventured to make to this answer to his manifesto was a tirade of abuse against the "Chronicle and Sentinel," which appeared in an Atlanta paper. Some of these peace editorials of Mr. Forrester found their way into the Northern papers, and excited much agreeable surprise at the boldness with which they assailed the Richmond Government and advocated a return to the Union, and a separate secession of Georgia herself from the Southern Confederacy. These efforts of Mr. Forrester in the cause of peace and re-union did much to dispose the Southern mind in favor of a return to the Union, and so alarming were they to Mr. Davis himself, that a warrant for the arrest of the publisher of the "Chronicle and Sentinel" was issued and attempted to be served, but was defeated by the interference of Gen. Beauregard, then in command at Augusta.

In 1862 he filled the post of Provost Marshal General, first of Western Tennessee, and afterwards of Northern Mississippi, having the rank of Colonel in the Confederate service, and being charged with the administration of martial law, which he administered for the protection and to the satisfaction of the people of those regions at a time of general disorder and suspension of civil law. While occupying this position Col. Forrester treated with remarkable kindness a large number of Union prisoners placed in his charge, his sanitary measures for the preservation of their health being so complete that scarcely a case of sickness and not a single death occurred among them. Many of these prisoners, both officers and privates, survive to attest the uniform courtesy and sympathy which marked their treatment. At this period exchanges of prisoners were freely made, and the harsh and cruel treatment of prisoners of war, which was afterwards adopted, had not been resorted to — a policy which received no sanction from Col. Forrester.

At the close of the year 1866, Col. Forrester was sent by the Confederate Secretary of War on a mission to Memphis, to negotiate an exchange of cotton for provisions, which President Lincoln had invited and encouraged, as tending to reconciliation and peace, by restoring commercial intercourse between the hostile sections. This mission was successful, Gen. Dana, then in command, giving to Col. Forrester a written order, guaranteeing from attack the steamer chartered to carry on the trade.

After the close of the war, Mr. Forrester retired to his cotton plantation in Alabama, on which he continued to reside, practicing his profession with distinction in the neighboring courts, until, in 1868, continued ill-health and the troubles of the country induced him to remove to Chicago, where he has since resided, devoting himself to the practice of law with a good measure of success, having gained a number of important revenue cases in the Circuit Court of the United States, and also a number of important causes in the Supreme Court of Illinois.

He has been a hard student in his time, and is extensively read in his profession. As a practitioner, he is regarded as zealously devoted to the interests of his clients, bringing to the management of his cases skill and persistent energy. He is a little over fifty years of age, and still in the prime of life.

CAROL GAYTES

Was born in Vermont; came West when a boy, and returned to the East for his education, graduating at Amherst College, where he acquired somewhat of a literary reputation. He became a resident of Chicago in 1864; commenced the practice of law in 1867; and, although a young man, he has already achieved considerable prominence from his devotion to his profession and his social excellences. He does a very successful business in the line of insurance, banking, bankruptcy, and commercial law; his counsels being sought, not alone for his legal opinions, but largely for his clear and practical business views. His judicious real estate operations have secured for him, early in life, a handsome fortune. He is president of a railroad company recently organized for the purpose of building a road through extensive coal and iron lands, in which he has large interests. Mr. Gaytes is a man of cultivation outside of his profession, and has a rare private library, which is especially rich in old, unique and valuable books. It is hoped by his friends that he will not suffer business pursuits to allure him from his profession, or to absorb his literary tastes and talents, which his means would now afford him leisure to cultivate to some purpose.

OBADIAH JACKSON.

Mr. Jackson is a native of Brooklyn, New York, and came to Chicago in 1841. He studied law with Scates, McAllister & Jewett, and was admitted to the bar in 1861. He then went into partnership with the firm with which he had studied. In time, Mr. Scates went into the army, and Judge McAllister retired, leaving the firm as it at present stands, that of Jewett & Jackson. Mr. Jackson is about thirty-three years of age, and is very popular among his acquaintances and the profession. He confines himself largely to real estate law and office business. He is a gentleman of brains and cultivation. He is a hard worker, a careful, pains-taking lawyer; and the result of his application to business is that he has secured a very handsome competence.

GEORGE CHANDLER.

Mr. Chandler is the junior member of the firm of Goudy & Chandler, and is a young man of promise. He is a very superior office lawyer, and prepares a case as well as the majority of older men of the profession in Chicago.

EDWARD MARTIN.

Mr. Martin bears the reputation of being a very superior chancery lawyer, and a most indefatigable worker. He is an Englishman by birth, and is about fifty years of age. He is exceedingly well read; as a speaker he is quite diffuse, but when he has finished the presentation of a case, but little more, if anything, pertinent to the issue remains unsaid.

W. H. HOLDEN.

This young lawyer is a student of Hon. Thos. Hoyne, and does credit to his instructor. He is a young man of decided ability, and promises, with age, to take a high rank in the legal profession.

KIRK HALL.

Mr. Hall is a young man of considerable promise, and who has in him many elements of great value. He is very industrious and energetic, has very clear legal perceptions, and is quite promising as a speaker. He is a hard worker, prepares a case very thoroughly, and, in time, will make a lawyer of a good deal more than average prominence.

GEORGE C. CAMPBELL.

Mr. Campbell is lately from Ottawa, where he was in partnership with Messrs. Glover & Cook. He is about forty years of age, is the attorney of the Chicago and Rock Island Railroad, is a very quiet gentleman, and a man of very fine capacity.

MRS. MYRA BRADWELL.

This lady is entitled to a place in this collection, in that she has studied law, and is at the head of the only legal journal of any value in the West. She was born in 1831, in Vermont. Early in life she removed to New York, and when thirteen years of age she came West, and has lived most of the time since in Chicago. She began the study of law fourteen years ago, and made application for admission to the bar in 1869. She was refused, and her case is now before the Supreme Court of the United States, having been taken there in regular process from one of the courts of this city. In October, 1868, she began the publication of "The Legal News," and through its columns she has shown herself a thinker and a writer of a very high order, and has amply demonstrated that her demand for admission to the bar is based upon a thorough knowledge of the requirements and duties of the legal profession.

She is of medium height, with fine, regular, sensitive features, an intelligent and womanly face, and black hair, and black, expressive eyes. She is a woman who is excellently well informed upon the current events of the day; is a superior conversationalist; and while she takes a fine rank as a legal thinker, she is no less successful in the direction of being an excellent mother, and a thoroughly estimable lady.

THOMAS S. McCLELLAND.

Thomas S. McClelland is one of the most promising of our rising young lawyers. He is a native of Pennsylvania, but removed to Illinois while quite young, and resided for some years in the central part of the State. He prepared for college at Beloit, Wisconsin, and also took the first three years of the regular collegiate course in that excellent institution, but spent his senior year at Williams' College.

where he graduated in 1864. He served in the army from December, 1864, to August, 1865, and then coming to Chicago, studied law with Hon. W. C. Goudy, was admitted to the bar in November, 1866, and commenced to practice June 1, 1867.

Mr. McClelland is a close student, a sound, clear-headed thinker, and a man of unusual integrity and stability of character. He is over six feet high, straight as an Indian, and almost as swarthy. He is about 33 years of age, and a bachelor. While well read in all departments of his profession, he pays somewhat special attention to corporation and real estate law, and is destined to take a high rank as a Chancery lawyer. He has conducted several important cases of this kind, involving heavy corporation interests, to successful termination, and has proved himself a safe counsellor and an able advocate.

J. C. KNICKERBOCKER.

Mr. Knickerbocker is a native of Columbia county, New York, and is now about thirty-five years of age. He studied law in Chicago and was admitted to the bar in 1862. He has been to the Legislature one term, and has held various municipal and county offices. His practice is a general one, with a large amount of probate business; and he is regarded as among the most promising of the younger members of the profession.

His brother J. J. Knickerbocker, is the junior member of the firm, and is also a young man of decided promise.

JAMES A. COWLES

Is a young man, a graduate of Union College, a very thorough and estimable gentleman. He makes a specialty of patent law, in which department of practice he is excellently well informed. He is indefatigable in application, and is a practitioner who deserves and meets with very substantial success.

FRANCIS LACKNER.

This gentleman is a German, and is a young man both of prominence and promise. He is a representative German lawyer, and in addition to his ability, he possesses a high order of character, and a very polished manner.

JULIUS ROSENTHAL.

Mr. Rosenthal is very proficient in probate law, is a very superior classical scholar, understands several modern languages, is Librarian of the Law Institute, a man of a very extended knowledge of books, and a young lawyer who is generally regarded as one of excellent promise.

JAMES LEDDY

Is twenty-six years of age. He studied law with Higgins and Swett, and was admitted to the bar five years ago. He is well thought of as a rising lawyer; he has a good deal of criminal business; is very energetic and industrious; has abundant self-possession, and is a speaker of more than average ability.

His brother, Thomas Leddy, junior, is thirty years of age. He studied law in Joliet, and was admitted in 1865. He has much promise, confines himself mainly to office business, and will probably make his mark as a counsellor in due season. While in Joliet he was City Attorney for two years.

EDWIN BEAN.

Is a native of New Hampshire, and has been a resident of Chicago since the year 1853. He originated here the collection agency now conducted by Bradstreet & Sons; his connection with which he relinquished for a position in the law firm of Helm, Clark & Bean. The extensive collection business of that firm and the succeeding one of Clark & Bean he conducted for upwards of ten years He is now a member of the firm of Wilkinson, Sackett and Bean. As a business lawyer, and in the department of collecting, he has no equal in extended experience and success.

U. F. LINDER.

This lawyer has now somewhat retired from law practice; and hence it needs only be said of him that, at one time, he was one of the most eloquent and powerful advocates in Chicago, and possibly in the Northwest.

KIRK D. PIERCE.

This gentleman, who is a recent comer to Chicago, is of Eastern birth, and a nephew of Ex-President Pierce. He is a lawyer of great promise; is thoroughly educated and only requires time to attain the greatest eminence in a profession which presents unlimited scope for the display of talent.

Mr. Pierce's personal appearance is favorable, and he is a speaker of considerable force and fluency. Among the many talented young men who are entering the legal profession, there are few, or none, who have a more brilliant augury for the future than Mr. Pierce.

ROBERT E. JENKINS.

Mr. Jenkins was born in Clark county, Missouri, in 1846, but spent the first ten years of his life in Iowa. At that age, he returned to his father, and for several years worked on the farm summers and attended school winters. He had the advantage, however, of a small but well selected library of History, Biography, and the Standard English poets to occupy his leisure hours, and this, with the natural taste for reading which he possessed, gave him a fair start in general education. He finally left the farm and entered the Illinois College at Jacksonville, Ill., but did not finish the course. In 1866 he came to Chicago and attended the Law School, from which he graduated in 1867. He was soon after admitted to the bar, and has since resided and practiced in Chicago. Mr. Jenkins confines himself chiefly to practice under the United States bankrupt law, and has made a successful specialty of this line of practice. He very frequently is called upon to act as assignee of bankrupt estates, being generally chosen by creditors rather than appointed by Court. The practice of bankruptcy law is intricate and attended with an unlimited amount of minute detail, which requires for its successful working a great deal of patience and hard work. Mr. Jenkins brings to the work just the painstaking, indefatigable industry which, judging from the position he has already achieved, will bring him into the ranks of successful lawyers.

MILTON T. PETERS.

This gentleman was born in Ohio, where his early boyhood was spent His early advantages were limited, and from an early age he was obliged to depend upon his own resources. At twenty-one he removed to Iowa, where he began practicing law, before he ever studied regularly. Being a man of great force of character, he soon became a proficient in the principles of law. He practiced and studied together until he was admitted to the bar. He removed to Princeton, Illinois, and practiced there acceptably; and in 1866 came to Chicago, where he has met with a fair amount of success. He was in partnership with Judge Wilkinson for a time, but finally went by himself, and carries on a lucrative practice of a general character.

Mr. Peters is a man of marked characteristics, and full of contradictions. He is bluff and harsh in manner and speech, while at heart he is full of kindliness and generosity. The nervous temperament predominates, and he is quick in action and speech. He possesses acute perceptions; is impulsive and often hasty in forming conclusions; but always is ready to make the *amende honorable* when convinced of an error. He is advanced in ideas, and is prominent among the Spiritualists and reformers of the day.

DANIEL D. DRISCOLL.*

This gentleman is the youngest son of Rev. Luther Driscoll, a Baptist clergyman, and who removed with his family to Illinois in 1837. Mr. Driscoll worked on a farm and attended the district school until sixteen years of age, when he commenced teaching. He also attended school during this period, and commenced the study of law with Hon. Julius Manning, who was then located in Knoxville in this State. Mr. Driscoll came to Chicago in 1854, but being in ill-health, and without means, he traveled for a time as collector for a city firm. Recovering his health, he opened a law office in 1857. During the succeeding ten years he formed partnerships with various gentlemen, and at the end of that period he was elected City Attorney, which office he filled for two years. He then formed a partnership with

* Deceased.

Mr. Jos. Pfirshing — a fine French and German scholar — with whom he still is.

Mr. Driscoll is thirty-eight years of age, and a tall, well-built gentleman, with light hair and beard, and gray eyes. He is the possessor of a very excellent knowledge of his profession, but he devotes himself more especially to the *rôle* of an advocate. He is a very effective jury lawyer, and has made speeches, such as in the Comstock-Grear case, and the Dent divorce suit, which have commanded a wide notice and admiration. He has a good deal of criminal business, in which he has achieved a very pronounced success.

His partner, Mr. Pfirshing, is a very fine scholar, and is a graduate of the Paris University, and also that at Heidelburg, Germany. Mr. Volney T. Kenney, the remaining partner, is a brother of Hon. Thos. J. Kenney, of Ashland, Ohio, and is a young man of more than ordinary promise in the legal profession.

NORMAN C. PERKINS.

Mr. Perkins was born in Pomfret, Vermont, in 1832. Was educated in the schools of his native town, and graduated at Yale College in 1857. In October of the same year Mr. Perkins came to Chicago and entered the office of George Scoville to study law. He was admitted to the bar in 1858, and has since resided in this city, engaged in the practice of his profession. Mr. Perkins is a fine-looking, genial gentleman, of cultivation, and socially is a great favorite. As a lawyer, he is well read, and inclined to concentrate his efforts on real estate law, though he is an excellent adviser and an able advocate in any branch of the profession.

JASPER D. WARD, ETC.

It is impossible that each of the one thousand lawyers of Chicago should receive detailed mention, unless in a work which should extend through several volumes. Hence there are many who must necessarily be omitted entirely, while there are others for whom there can be no more done than barely to allude to their names. Among this class there are many excellent lawyers who deserve more space, but which act of justice is forbidden by the limits of this publication. Among those who should recive more than a passing notice are JASPER D. WARD, an ex-Senator of the Illinois Legislature, and a citizen of prominence; GEORGE H. WINSTON, who was formerly a prominent railroad attorney; H. K. WHITON, who is from Wisconsin, and the partner of Joseph A. Sleeper; GEORGE F. BAILEY, who was the partner of Judge Gary, and is a young man who bears a good reputation; H. B. HURD, formerly of Hurd, Booth & Cramer; JOHN W. BENNETT, who is a very promising young lawyer; JOHN A. HUNTER, who is very highly mentioned by the older members of the bar; TELFORD BURNHAM, who has fine abilities, and a large amount of dash and vigor; DAVID B. LYMAN, who is a young gentleman of good abilities; R. W. BRIDGE, who is a *protegé* of Gookins & Roberts, and who possesses very fair ability; L. S. HODGES, a reputable and hard-working lawyer; DAVID QUIGG, the junior of Higgins, Swett & Quigg, a young man of the most decided ability and promise; ANDREW GARRISON, who is one of the oldest lawyers in Chicago, and a highly respected practitioner; IRA W. BUELL, ex-City Attorney, and a very clever lawyer; F. B. PEABODY, who was formerly very prominent as a real estate lawyer; S. K. DOW; GEORGE W. STANFORD; JOSEPH N. BARKER, partner of M. F. Tuley; JOHN BORDEN, a very accurate and acute real estate lawyer, who is very highly respected; NORMAN WILLIAMS, junior, a young man who promises well for the future; JAMES H. KNOWLTON; CYRUS BENTLEY, from Wisconsin, who has established himself as a gentleman of a high order of abilities; L. A. COLBURN, who is well known as a patent-law practitioner; HORATIO G. SPAFFORD: ROBERT M. WILSON, ex-Recorder, and who is a very effective jury lawyer; W. C. GRANT, formerly a partner of Williams, Woodbridge & Grant, and who stands well and has a fine practic; GEORGE W. THOMPSON; E. S. BRAGG, who is an ex-military officer, a late arrival from Wisconsin, and who carries in his practice all the precision and accuracy of a military drill; JOHN MATTOX, who is a gentleman that occupies a quite prominent legal position; SIMEON W. KING, who is Commissioner of all the States and Territories, and who has worked his way into the profession solely by his own energy; J. A. J. KENDIG, a gentleman of fine social, and some excellent professional attainments; S. B. PERRY, an old practitioner and of very fair standing in the profession; JOHN C. ROBERTS, a very careful and pains-taking lawyer, and managing member of the firm of Gookins & Roberts; H. N. HIBBARD, who is Register in Bankruptcy, who is a very excellent lawyer; JAMES L. HIGH, who is a self-made young man, modest, quiet demeanor, an industrious worker, a good lawyer, and an author and editor of some note; L. H. BOUTELL, for some years the assistant and moving spirit in the office of the United States District Attorney; S. A. IRWIN, who is a shrewd manager, a man of a good deal of influence, a very excellent lawyer, at present Collector of Internal Revenue, and while City Attorney achieved creditable success; FRANCIS ADAMS, who is a quiet gentleman, a lawyer of more than average ability, and was once City Attorney; F. H. KALES, who is a partner of Judge Beckwith, and a very shrewd, adroit, keen and thoroughly well-read member of the legal profession; S. B. GOOKINS, who sustains a very fine reputation in his character as a lawyer and as a private citizen, and occupies a very influential position in every respect in this community, who is an ex-judge, and senior of the firm of Gookins & Roberts; Col. THOMAS GROSVENOR, formerly attorney of the Police Courts, an intelligent, affable, and popular young man, who was shot by a guard at the time the city was under military control, during the week following the fire; AUGUSTUS VAN BUREN, who does a large amount of police business; T. HENRY TRUMAN, a young man who has traveled extensively in Europe and elsewhere, and who is possessed of a great amount of energy, nerve and ability, and is a young lawyer of unusal thoroughness and excellence; H. S. TOWLE, junior of Goodwin, Larnard & Towle, who is regarded as a young man of much promise, who has a fine education and considerable experience; W. F. WHITEHOUSE, a young gentleman of polished address and great industry; WM. P. BLACK, of Dent & Black, a gentleman who is very highly spoken of;

CHARLES M. HARRIS, an ex-member of Congress, a clear thinker, and a very honest, conscientious man; DANIEL J. AVERY, who is a partner of E. F. Runyan, and is a lawyer of promise, which may also be said of E. F. COMSTOCK, who is also a partner in the same firm, and who is looked upon as a rising young man; J. EDWARDS FAY, of Bonney, Fay, & Griggs, a very good real estate and business lawyer, and has been a resident of Chicago about eleven years; CHARLES W. GRIGGS, of the same firm, who is accurate in his reading and practice, and a young lawyer of unusual promise; JAMES L. STARK, who has very much more ability than he is popularly credited with, whose practice is a good one, and whose qualities both as a man and a lawyer are of a very high order; JOSIAH H. BISSELL, who has lately been appointed reporter for the Seventh Judicial District, is a young man of promise in his profession, and possesses a clear, acute mind, excellent judgment, and has an extended knowledge of the practical requirements of his profession, which will greatly assist him in his new position; GEORGE F. HARDING, who is a fine lawyer, whose specialty is real estate, and who is withal a capital business manager, and a man who stands well with the community, and the members of his profession; CARTER H. HARRISON, J. B. VAUGHAN, and many others.

There are many gentlemen of great prominence who do not properly belong to the bar of Chicago, but who are, or who have been, connected with it incidentally, or by indirection. Among these may be mentioned:

LYMAN TRUMBULL, United States Senator, ex-Judge of the Supreme Court of Illinois, who occupies a very high rank as a lawyer, and who is distinguished for the clearness and force of his judicial opinions.

JAMES R. DOOLITTLE, who obtained pre-eminence as a Wisconsin lawyer and judge; was a United States Senator from that State; and who developed fine ability as a constitutional lawyer in the impeachment of Andrew Johnson.

JOHN M. WILSON, who was for a long time the Chancellor and Chief Justice of the Superior Court; is now President of the South Park Commission, and who was justly regarded as one of the most eminent lawyers in the Northwest, and one of the best judges who ever occupied a judicial bench in Chicago.

GEORGE TRUMBULL, a very quiet, unpretending, well-read and able lawyer, for a time successor of John M. Douglas, an attorney of the Illinois Central railroad.

JOHN M. DOUGLAS, who is very widely known for many years as the President and chief counsellor of the Illinois Central railroad company. He is a man of commanding judgment and high administrative abilities.

JOHN D. CATON, who was widely distinguished as one of the Chief Justices of the Supreme Court in this State. He is a man of great learning, and has taken a very high judicial rank.

N. B. JUDD, who was Member of Congress for several terms, Minister to Berlin, and who, had it not been for his absorption by politics, would have attained distinction as a lawyer.

WALTER B. SCATES, who was for a long time one of the Justices, and for a while Chief Justice of the Supreme Court of this State, and who has, since his descent from the bench, been Collector of the Port in this city, and is now on the retired list of Chicago lawyers.

MARK SKINNER, L. C. P., FREER, BUCKNER S. MORRIS and E. B. HOOPER are all men who once were actively engaged in the practice of law, but who, having acquired fortunes in this direction, are now no longer engaged in the active duties of the legal profession.

The courts have taken away some excellent men from the bar of this city. They are as follows:

W. K. McALLISTER, of the Supreme Court for the Chicago District, a sketch of whom appears in another place.

E. S. WILLIAMS, Chief Justice of the Circuit Court, who has a very wide reputation for his patience, learning, great urbanity, and for his inflexible official rectitude.

JOHN G. ROGERS is Associate Justice of the Circuit Court, one of the lately elected officials, who is a gentleman of very finished manners, of impressive presence, who has a superior judicial mind, and who will doubtless distinguish the position which he occupies.

W. H. FARWELL, Associate Justice of the Circuit Court, who occupies the Chancellor's bench of that court with Judge Williams, and who is a quiet, unpretentious gentleman, and has a well-informed, judicial mind.

HENRY BOOTH, also Associate Justice in the Circuit Court, who has long been distinguished as the head of the law department of Douglas University, and who brings to the bench a very wide range of legal scholarship.

JOHN A. JAMESON, Chief Justice and Chancellor of the Superior Court, who is an exceedingly patient and industrious student, has produced a valuable treatise on constitutional conventions, and is editor of the "Law Register." He is probably more widely known than any other of our State judges.

JOSEPH E. GARY, Associate Justice of the same court, who is remarkable for his disposition of business, and who, in the trial of causes, displays an amount of knowledge seldom exhibited in the same position.

WM. A. PORTER, also Associate Justice in the same court, who is a man of imposing presence, of pleasing manners, and who occupies the law bench of the Superior Court with Judge Gary.

M. R. M. WALLACE, of the Probate Court, who is a very conscientious, patient and pains-taking official, and whose convictions of right are sincere, and apparent to all who come before him.

DAVID DAVIS, Supreme Judge of the United States Court, and who has the reputation of having more common sense than any man in the United States. He rose from the State court to his present position at one promotion. He is thoroughly grounded in common law and chancery systems, and enjoys a very wide consideration.

THOMAS DRUMMOND, United States District Judge of the Chicago District, who enjoys a very enviable reputation, has great learning, extended experience, and was made District Judge by a unanimous choice

H. W. BLODGETT, Circuit Judge of the Chicago Circuit of the United States Court, who, before taking his present position, was long and favorably known as a railroad lawyer and a State Senator. He has been a very hard student, and now gives very general satisfaction.

IRA SCOTT, Master in Chancery of the Superior Court, who is one of the most experienced Masters in Chancery in the State. Next to him are JOHN WOODBRIDGE, of the Circuit Court, and H. W. BISHOP, of the United States Court, and who are all gentlemen who adequately fill their positions.

Chicago has produced a good many men who occupied distinguished positions at this bar, but who are now dead. Prominent among these were:

ALFRED W. ARRINGTON, a grand intellect and a poet; E. W. TRACY, who was one of the most brilliant and intellectual men ever known to the profession in Chicago; PAT BALLINGALL, who acted as Prosecuting Attorney for a number of years, and was a very social and noted man; DAN. McELROY, also a very social and genial gentleman; LYLE SMITH, who was an orator, and possessed the highest kind of eloquence, was social, and always ready for a speech on any occasion; JUSTIN BUTTERFIELD, who is said to have possessed more brains than any of his compeers, was a friend of Webster, and of a Websterian class of intellect, and who held several public offices of importance for many years; JAMES H. COLLINS, who was a fine lawyer, and who, in connection with Butterfield, had nearly all the practice at this bar; GILES SPRING, who was a judge of the Circuit Court, and a first-class lawyer in every respect, an excellent judge, and a relative of the well-known Dr. Spring, of New York; RICHARD S. THOMAS, who was very prominent as a real estate lawyer; JOHN A. BROWN; RICHARD HAMILTON; THEOPHILUS SMITH; JESSE B. THOMAS; GEORGE MANNIERE; and GEORGE MEEKER.

THERE are legal gentlemen of prominence connected with towns immediately adjoining Chicago, some of whom sometimes appear in the courts of this city.

OTTAWA furnishes such men as T. Lyle Dickey, who served with distinction during the war, and who was once United States Assistant Attorney, and who is a man of very superior legal ability, without very great learning, but who is a natural lawyer; Washington Bushnell, who is now attorney General of the State, and who has clear judgment, and who, without being a great man, is well-developed in all that constitutes a lawyer; Burton C. Cook, who is a man of great shrewdness and versatility, and while not prominent as a speaker, is a good deal of a manager; and other gentlemen whose names must be omitted.

ELGIN contains the widely-known Colonel Edward S. Joslyn, who is forty-five years of age, of a very genial and social disposition, and who is an advocate whose eloquence is almost without a rival in the Northwest; Colonel John S. Wilcox, whose age is about thirty-eight, who is a cultivated gentleman, an evenly and well-developed lawyer, a good manager, and an industrious, pains-taking professional; Major A. H. Barry, who is forty-three years of age, and a fine jury lawyer; and Judge R. N. Botsford, who is thirty-eight years of age, a hard student, and a very competent office lawyer.

JOLIET has a large legal force, among whom may be mentioned Hon. Josiah McRoberts and Hon. G. D. A. Parks, who are both men of cultivation and scholarly tastes, with fine legal minds; Hon. S. W. Randall, an old citizen, and formerly of the Circuit Court; Frank Goodspeed, who was a prominent candidate for the Supreme bench; T. L. Breckinridge, a very ready and eloquent speaker; Benjamin Olin, who although a young man, has already won a very commanding position; Egbert Phelps, a scholarly young gentleman, with very fine poetical and literary tastes, and excellent legal abilities; Charles A. Hill, the District Attorney, who is a young man, and is rapidly rising in his profession; and S. W. Munn and E. C. Fellows, both of whom have attained distinction in the department of criminal law practice.

AURORA furnishes several conspicuous members of the legal profession, among whom the most prominent are Hon. B. F. Parks, R. G. Montony, and C. J. Metzner.

GENEVA has a reputable bar, of whom the best known are A. M. Harrington, formerly United States District Attorney for Northern Illinois, Hon. Wm. B. Plato, who is regarded as a counsellor of a very able kind.

INDEX.

Name	PAGE
ADAMS, FRANCIS	120
ANTHONY, ELLIOT	80
ARNOLD, ISAAC N.	58
ARRINGTON, ALFRED W.	124
ASAY, E. G.	47
ATWOOD, JULIUS P.	99
AVERY, DANIEL J.	121
AYER, B. F.	53
BATES, GEORGE C.	61
BAILEY, GEORGE F.	119
BARKER, JOSEPH N.	119
BALLINGALL, PAT	124
BARRY, MAJOR A. H.	125
BECKWITH, CORYDON	15
BEAN, EDWIN	115
BENNETT, JOHN W.	119
BENTLEY, CYRUS	119
BISSELL, JOSIAH H.	121
BISHOP, H. W.	124
BLODGETT, H. W.	124
BLACK, WILLIAM P.	120
BONNEY, CHARLES CARROLL	34
BONFIELD, JOSEPH F.	101
BOND, LESTER L.	107
BORDEN, JOHN	119
BOUTELL, L. H.	120
BOOTH, HENRY	123
BOTTSFORD, JUDGE R. N.	125
BRADWELL, JAMES B.	78
BRADWELL, MRS. MYRA	113
BRIDGE, R, W.	119
BRAGG, E. S.	120
BROWN, JOHN A.	124
BRECKENRIDGE, T. L.	125
BURNHAM, TELFORD	119
BUELL, IRA W.	119
BUTTERFIELD, JUSTIN	124
BUSHNELL, WASHINGTON	125
CAULFIELD, BERNARD G.	103
CAMPBELL, GEORGE C.	113
CATON, JOHN D.	122
CHANDLER, GEORGE	112
CLARKSON, JOSEPH P.	79
COWLES, JAMES A.	114
COLBURN, L. A.	119
COMSTOCK, E. F.	121
COLLINS, JAMES H.	124
COOK, BURTON C.	125
CRAM, J. A.	106
DAVIS, DAVID	123
DEXTER, WIRT	44
DENT, THOMAS	49
DICKEY, T. LYLE	125
DOOLITTLE, JAMES R.	122
DOUGLAS, JOHN M.	122
DOW, S. K.	119
DRISCOLL, DANIEL D.	118
DRUMMOND, THOMAS	124
ELA, JOHN W.	82
ELDRIDGE, HAMILTON N.	88
EVANS, E. W.	92
FAY, J. EDWARDS	121
FARWELL, W. H.	123
FELLOWS, E. C.	125
FORRESTER, ROBERT	109
FREER, C. P.	123
FULLER, SAMUEL W.	18
FULLER, MELVILLE W.	51
GARDINER, GEORGE	108
GAYTES, CAROL	111
GARRISON, ANDREW	119
GARY, JOSEPH E.	123
GOUDY, WILLIAM C.	13
GOODWIN, STEPHEN A.	56
GOODRICH, GRANT	71
GOODWIN, DANIEL, JR.	84
GOODWIN, DANIEL	86
GOOKINS, S. B.	120
GOODSPEED, FRANK	125
GRANT, W. C.	119
GROSVENOR, COL. THOMAS	120
GRIGGS, CHARLES M.	121
HALL, KIRK	112
HARRIS, CHARLES M.	120
HARDING, GEORGE F.	121
HARRISON, CARTER H.	121
HAMILTON, RICHARD	124
HARRINGTON, A. M.	126
HERVEY, ROBERT	21
HERBERT, GEORGE	74
HIGGINS, VAN H.	32
HITCHCOCK, CHARLES	37
HILL, EDWARD J.	87
HIGH, JAMES L.	120
HILL, CHARLES A.	125
HIBBARD, H. N.	120
HOYNE, THOMAS	9
HOYNE, PHILIP	104
HORTON, OLIVER H.	104
HOLDEN, W. H.	112
HODGES, L. S.	119
HOOPER, E. B.	123
HURD, H. B.	119
HUNTER, JOHN A.	119
IRWIN, S. A.	120
JACKSON, OBADIAH	111
JAMESON, JOHN A.	123
JEWETT, JOHN N.	29

Name	PAGE	Name	PAGE
JENKINS, ROBERT E.	116	ROBY, EDWARD	76
JOSLYN, COL. EDWARD S.	125	ROBERTS, JAMES H.	103
JUDD, N. B.	122	ROSENTHAL, JULIUS	115
KALES, F. H.	120	ROGERS, JOHN G.	123
KENDIG, J. A. J.	120	ROBERTS, JOHN C.	120
KING, WILLIAM H.	42	RUNYAN, E. F.	80
KING, JOHN LYLE	81	SACKETT, FREDERICK	108
KING, SIMEON W.	120	SCATES, WALTER B.	122
KNOX, JOSEPH	7	SCHUYLER, DANIEL J.	102
KNICKERBOCKER, J. C.	114	SCOTT, IRA	124
KNOWLTON, JAMES H.	119	SHOREY, D. L.	68
LARNED, EDWIN C.	100	SHERMAN, E. B.	72
LAWRENCE, A. H.	100	SKINNER, MARK	123
LACKNER, FRANCIS	114	SLEEPER, JOSEPH A.	103
LEAKE, JOSEPH B.	69	SMITH, SIDNEY	40
LE MOYNE, JOHN V.	96	SMITH, U. P.	104
LEDDY, JAMES	115	SMITH, LYLE	124
LINCOLN, ROBERT F.	105	SMITH, THEOPHILUS	124
LINDER, U. F.	115	SNOWHOOK, WM. B.	66
LYON, D. J.	106	SPRING, GILES	124
LYMAN, DAVID B.	119	SPAFFORD, HORATIO G.	119
MAGRUDER, BENJAMIN D.	73	STORRS, EMORY A.	54
MASON, JOHN	108	STILES, ISRAEL N.	63
MARTIN, EDWARD	112	STANFORD, GEORGE W.	119
MATTOX, JOHN	120	STARK, JAMES L.	121
MANNIERE, GEORGE	124	SWETT, LEONARD	24
MCALLISTER, WILLIAM K.	5	TENNEY, D. K.	100
MCCLELLAND, THOMAS S.	113	THOMPSON, JOHN L.	102
MCELROY, DAN	124	THOMPSON, GEORGE W.	120
MCKINNON, JOHN J.	96	THOMAS, RICHARD S.	124
MCROBERTS, HON. JOSIAH	125	THOMAS, JESSE B.	124
METZNER, C. J.	126	TOURTELLOTTE, F. W.	90
MEEKER, GEORGE	124	TOWLE, H. S.	120
MILLER, H. G.	30	TREE, LAMBERT	67
MONROE, HENRY S.	75	TRUMAN, T. HENRY	120
MOORE, SAMUEL M.	97	TRUMBULL, LYMAN	122
MORRIS, BUCKNER S.	123	TRUMBULL, GEORGE	122
MONTONY, R. S.	126	TRACY, E. W.	124
MUNN, S. W.	125	TULEY, M. F.	43
OLIN, BENJAMIN	125	TURNER, THOS. J.	94
PARKER, THOMAS, JR.	81	VAN ARMAN, JOHN	27
PARKS, HON. B. F.	126	VAN BUREN, EVARTS	78
PARKS, HON. G. D. A.	125	VAN BUREN, AUGUSTUS	120
PERKINS, MARLAND L.	85	VAUGHN, J. B.	121
PECK, JOHN H.	98	WALKER, JAMES M.	22
PERKINS, NORMAN C.	117	WARD, JASPER D.	119
PETERS, MILTON T.	117	WALLACE, M. R. M.	123
PEABODY, F. B.	119	WHITEHOUSE, WM. FITZ HUGH	120
PERRY, S. B.	120	WHITON, H. K.	119
PHELPS, S. D.	106	WILKINSON, IRA O.	62
PHELPS, EGBERT	125	WILSON, ISAAC G.	83
PLATO, HON. W. B.	126	WINDETT, A. W.	99
PIERCE, KIRK D.	116	WINSTON, GEO. H.	119
PORTER, WILLIAM A.	123	WILLIAMS, NORMAN, JR.	119
QUIGG, DAVID	119	WILSON, ROBERT M.	119
RAE, ROBERT	106	WILSON, JOHN M.	122
RANDALL, HON. S. W.	125	WILLIAMS, E. S.	123
REED, CHARLES H.	65	WILCOX, COL. JOHN S.	125
RICHARDSON, WILLIAM H.	97	WOODBRIDGE, JOHN	124

www.ingramcontent.com/pod-product-compliance
Lightning Source LLC
Chambersburg PA
CBHW031619170426
43195CB00037B/1147